Workplace Moods and Emotions: A Review of Research

Peter Totterdell[1] & Karen Niven[2]

[1]University of Sheffield, England
[2]University of Manchester, England

ISBN: 1495230430

ISBN-13:   978-1495230431

Cite as:

Totterdell, P., & Niven, K. (2014). *Workplace moods and emotions: A review of research*. Charleston, SC: Createspace Independent Publishing.

Correspondence:

Correspondence concerning this article should be addressed to Peter Totterdell, Department of Psychology, University of Sheffield, Sheffield S10 2TN, UK. Telephone +44(0)114 222 3234. Electronic mail may be sent to p.totterdell@sheffield.ac.uk.

Acknowledgements:

This research was funded by ESRC UK grant RES-060-25-0044: "Emotion regulation of others and self (EROS)".

About The Authors

Peter Totterdell is a Professor in the Psychology Department at Sheffield University, UK, and a Fellow of the British Psychological Society. Much of his research focuses on studying emotion in applied settings. He has published over 70 journal papers, as well as books and book chapters. Peter led the UK ESRC-funded large grant 'Emotion Regulation of Others and Self' (2008-2013). For more details see http://www.erosresearch.org

Karen Niven is a Lecturer in Organisational Psychology at Manchester Business School, Manchester University, UK. Her research focuses on the ways that people try to control their own and particularly others' emotions. She is interested in what drives these attempts to control emotion and what consequences these attempts have for people's lives. Karen has conducted studies in various social settings, including workplaces, romantic relationships, peer groups, and prisons, to explore these issues.

Workplace Moods and Emotions:
A Review of Research

Peter Totterdell and Karen Niven

Abstract

This review examines the nature, causes and consequences of momentary affect at work. It focuses on two major categories of affect: moods and discrete emotions. The review begins by explaining the nature of momentary affect and why it is important to study within-person fluctuations in affect. Following that it describes major theories and methods that facilitate research on momentary affect in the workplace, especially affective events theory and time-sampling methods. Next, the review examines the empirical evidence concerning the characteristics of the worker and the work environment that cause momentary mood, and the consequences of momentary mood for workers' affective response, satisfaction, cognitive performance, behavior and relationships. It then reviews the evidence for the causes and consequences of discrete emotions, including anger and envy. Finally, the review identifies some questions that future research on momentary affect needs to address in the form of ten challenges.

Introduction

Imagine that someone approaches you at work and asks how you feel. What might you report feeling, what would have led you to feel that way, and what consequences would those feelings have for you and your work? In this account we will review what research tells us in answer to these questions. Our focus is on feelings experienced in the moment, although as we shall explain later this has often entailed researchers examining feelings pertaining to longer periods of time. Feelings experienced in the here and now are known as momentary affect, and in this review we will examine the nature, causes and consequences of momentary affect at work. In particular we will focus on two major categories of affect: moods and discrete emotions. So we will begin by explaining the nature of momentary affect, including the distinction between moods and discrete emotions. We will then describe some psychological theories and methods that are facilitating research on this topic. Following this, we will address moods and then discrete emotions, reviewing empirical evidence concerning their causes and consequences. Finally, we will identify some questions for future research to address concerning momentary affect at work.

Nature of Momentary Affect

In a recent review article concerning research on emotion in organizational behavior, Ashkanasy and Humphrey (2011) presented a multi-level model of emotion in organizations in which research at the first of five levels involves studying within-person emotion. They explain that at this level, "the focus is on momentary temporal variations in within-person emotion as experienced by individual organizational members" (p. 215). The present review is primarily concerned with research at this level of analysis. It encompasses individuals' emotional reactions to events that occur at work, and how those reactions determine attitudinal and behavioral outcomes. This territory was first mapped out by affective events theory (Weiss and Cropanzano, 1996), of which we will say more later. The other levels in the Ashkanasy and Humphrey (2011) model concern between-person variation, interpersonal variation, group or team variation, and organizational variation.

Affective experience can be divided into a number of subcategories which include mood, emotion, and affective well-being. Moods are temporary but longer lasting and more diffuse than emotions, and unlike emotions are typically not directed at any specific event. Examples of moods include feeling calm, tense, and enthusiastic. Emotions are made up of a number of components, including the type of reaction involved (e.g., physiological response), appraisal (e.g., goal relevance), and behavior of response (e.g., facial expression). Examples of emotions include feeling angry, frightened, disgusted and proud. Affective well-being is more enduring and generalised than moods and emotions and may be an outcome of these more temporary states, so it will not be considered further in this review. However, some feelings appear in all three categories. For example, feeling happy has been conceived as a mood, an emotion, and as affective well-being.

A number of other constructs that involve momentary affect have also been studied in organizations. These include: vigor which refers to feelings of having physical strength, emotional energy, and cognitive liveliness (Shirom, 2001); state work engagement which refers to a state of pleasurable activation involving vigor, dedication, and absorption (Schaufeli & Bakker, 2010); and flow which has been conceptualized as the pleasure derived from acting with total involvement and comprises a number of elements including absorption and intrinsic motivation (Csikszentmihalyi & LeFevre, 1989). Given that these states have elements that are additional to affect, we will exclude them from current consideration except in their overlap with the relevant mood or emotion.

Research on the structure of affective experience divides into researchers who use models such as the circumplex model which characterise moods and emotions in terms of the extent to which they involve underlying dimensions such as pleasantness and activation (e.g., calmness = high pleasure, low activation), and those who use models which place emotions into discrete categories that contain irreducible basic emotions from which more complex emotions are derived (Cropanzano, Weiss, Hale, & Reb, 2003). Disagreements still exist as to whether these models are the most appropriate for representing affect (e.g., Feldman-Barrett et al., 2007). Nevertheless, these two conceptions have spawned different lines of research and hence we will review research on moods and discrete emotions in organizations in separate sections later in the review.

Is a focus on momentary affect warranted? When affect is measured over different time periods, it is clear that while averaged momentary experiences of affect correspond to affect reported for the time period that incorporates those experiences, there also differences; for example, longer time-frames are more sensitive to concurrent mood and tend to indicate that affect is more positive (e.g., Parkinson, Briner, Reynolds, & Totterdell, 1995). It is also warranted because results based on time-point comparisons can be different to those based on person comparisons. A good example of this is the correlation between satisfaction and performance, which is usually weak when looking at whether workers who are more satisfied with their jobs perform better (Judge & Bono, 2001), but stronger when looking at whether workers perform better at times when they feel more satisfied with their work tasks (Fisher, 2003).

There would however be little point in studying affect over short timescales if it did not fluctuate over short periods of time, such as within a work day or between work days. Studies in different occupational settings have demonstrated considerable within-person variation in affect across different timescales, including within-day (e.g., Miner, Glomb & Hulin, 2005), between-days (e.g., Williams & Alliger, 1994), and between-weeks (e.g., Totterdell, Wood, & Wall, 2006). Fisher (2002) found that as much as 47% of the variance in positive momentary affective reactions and 77% of the variance in negative affective reactions at work occurred within rather than between persons, and was not therefore due to individual differences. This variation also cannot be explained by differences between work environments, because these are too stable, which suggests that it arises from the events that people encounter during their work days, and how they experience those events.

As well as ascertaining what a person feels at work at any given time, it may also be important to consider how work is experienced from the individual's point of view in order to understand its affective meaning (Weiss & Rupp, 2011). Beal and Weiss (2013) propose that goal-based episodes are the appropriate framework for understanding how the various elements of daily experience interconnect. In their view, people partition their everyday experiences into episodic segments that are organised around personal goals. They refer to the segments as performance episodes when the goals are organizationally relevant. A segment may have an associated affect. For example, a work meeting may have a feeling attached to it. In contrast, discrete emotion episodes are seen as being organized around instigating events and provide the experiential aspect of experience, but not its temporal structure. Understanding the basis on which people chunk their continuous temporal experience of work into meaningful episodes poses a difficult but important research challenge. What is clear, however, is that studying momentary affect cannot be restricted to investigating the present moment only.

Understanding and Studying Momentary Affect

Theories for Understanding Momentary Affect

As we mentioned in the previous section, affective events theory (AET; Weiss & Cropanzano, 1996) provided the first major framework for studying the causes, structure, and consequences (attitudinal and behavioral) of affective experiences at work. The theory focuses on how affective experiences unfold in response to events at work. According to the theory, behavior is either a direct response to an affective experience (*affect-driven behavior*) or an indirect response mediated by a work attitude such as job satisfaction (*judgment-driven behavior*). Affect-driven behavior is more spontaneous and requires less cognitive processing, whereas judgment-driven behavior requires consideration of the situation followed by a decision to behave in a particular way. It follows from this distinction that affect will be more strongly associated with affect-driven behavior than judgment-driven behavior because the latter is only indirectly associated with affect via work attitudes. The theory also emphasises the importance of studying temporal process, and the episodic structure of discrete emotions.

Weiss and Brief (2001) identified four key elements of AET, that it: 1) makes a distinction between affect and satisfaction, because satisfaction is seen as an evaluation of a job rather than an affective reaction to it; 2) emphasises events as a causal influence on affect; 3) views affect as having an immediate influence on performance; and 4) makes a distinction between affect-driven and judgment-driven behavior. Reflecting later on the research utility of AET, Weiss and Beal (2005) emphasised that AET provides an organizing framework for research rather than a testable theoretical explanation, even though it contains some testable hypotheses. With respect to the key elements of AET, Weiss and Beal (2005) concluded that: the few studies that had compared job affect and satisfaction were supportive of the distinction; research had identified the influence of a wide range of work events on affect (especially negative events); but there was insufficient existing evidence concerning the proposed distinction between affect- and judgment-driven behaviors. More broadly, they found that although research on work had increased its attention to within-person changes in affect and discrete emotions, it had not advanced with respect to reflecting the episodic nature of work experience or in specifying the processes involved in AET. In a more recent summary, Ashkanasy and Humphrey (2011) concluded that empirical research based on AET had been invariably supportive of the theory and they noted how it was now being used to account for a wider range of behaviors, including counterproductive work behavior. AET is also being used to advance understanding in other areas of organizational behavior, such as leadership behavior (Walter & Bruch, 2009).

Research has also now begun to specify some of the processes involved in AET. More precisely, researchers have begun to marry AET with other theories that have already expanded on the psychological mechanisms involved in some of its causal paths. Ashton-James and Ashkanasy (2005), for example, used an affect regulation model to explain how affective events generate affect and how affect influences behavior. The model has two systems, the first of which generates affective responses through perception and assimilation of affective information, and the second of which regulates the affective response through emotion understanding and management. These processes correspond to Lazarus's (1991) appraisal processes, and also map on to components in Mayer and Salovey's (1997) model of emotional intelligence. The idea is that how a worker behaves in response to a work event depends on the affect the event generates and how that affect is self-regulated. The affect is controlled both through cognition (e.g., reappraisal) and through behavior (e.g., coping), and success in controlling the affect is continually monitored and the behaviour adjusted accordingly.

In relation to job performance, AET does not specify the information processing mechanisms by which affect influences performance. However, there is a wealth of research on the cognitive effects of affect and a range of plausible models to draw on. For example, Forgas's (1995) affect infusion model – which proposes that moods have most influence on tasks that require elaborate processing – is able to explain why workers are likelier to take greater risks when in a positive mood (Ashkanasy & Humphrey, 2011). AET can therefore be used in conjunction with more focused theories to explain the consequences of momentary affect.

There is, however, a potential challenge to a central tenet of AET, which has not yet percolated through to organizational research. AET is based on the premise that feelings drive behavior. However, Baumeister, Vohs, DeWall, and Zhang (2007) argue that while direct causation does sometimes occur, it is more common for behaviors to pursue anticipated feelings. Evidence for this view has come from studies showing that people's usual behavior in response to a mood can be stopped by leading them to believe that their mood is frozen (e.g., Manucia, Baumann, & Cialdini, 1984). Baumeister et al. (2007) have proposed a feedback model as an alternative to the direct causation model. In this model, individuals use past affective experience to anticipate how they would feel were they to follow particular courses of action and then choose behaviors that they believe will attain the feelings they desire. The actual experience that follows from the behavior then guides future behavior. For example, in a work context, workers would make daily decisions about their work behavior based on anticipating how they would feel if they acted that way. The anticipated feeling would be based on feedback from past experiences at work. The feedback model therefore offers a potentially insightful framework for explaining learning at work, and in particular how momentary affect could shape learned behavior, but empirical evidence in work settings is required.

Methods for Studying Momentary Affect

Investigating how affect varies during work-time has required the development of appropriate methods because traditional methods such as workplace surveys are unable to capture events and experiences as they occur. Briner and Kiefer (2009) noted that research on organizational affect has largely neglected event-based methods in favour of methods that are incongruent with theory concerning the time-course of emotions. Fortunately, a number of methods have been developed that do enable researchers to collect data from workers on numerous occasions over a period of time. These time-sampling methods go by various names, such as diary methods, experience-sampling, and ecological momentary assessment (e.g., Alliger & Williams, 1993; Beal & Weiss, 2003).

These methods enable an in-depth study of everyday experiences and ongoing behavior in its natural environment (Csikszentmihalyi & Larson, 1987) and are ideally suited to identifying the situational and personal conditions that give rise to variations in affect at work, and to studying the consequences of those variations. Although use of these methods has only blossomed in the last two decades, one of the first studies to use a time-sampling method in an organization was reported by Hersey as long as 80 years ago (Hersey, 1932). Hersey asked a group of factory workers to record their emotions a number of times a day for up to a year, and used this data to extract patterns in their affect and to identify how their affect related to work events and performance.

Study designs using time-sampling methods can be categorized into signal-, interval- or event-contingent (Wheeler & Reis, 1991). Signal-contingent designs require participants to report on their current experience when prompted by a signal, sent on a fixed or quasi-random schedule. Interval-contingent designs also signal participants but require them to report on their experiences since the last signal (usually sent at equal intervals). The sampling-rate varies but is usually either several times a day or daily. More frequent sampling minimizes inaccuracies arising from biases in memory recall. Finally, event-contingent designs require participants to report on their experiences whenever a pre-specified event occurs (e.g., a work meeting).

There are various options available to the researcher for signaling participants and recording data during such studies. Early studies were restricted to using pagers and watch alarms for signaling and paper booklets for recording, but researchers can now use palmtop computers or cell phones for both signaling and recording. An alternative method for collecting data that can be used is the reconstruction method which prompts participants to re-experience episodes using episodic memory traces that access the momentary experiences. This method can be used to reconstruct days (Kahneman, Krueger, Schkade, Schwarz, & Stone, 2004) or events (Grube, Schroer, Hentzschel, & Hertel, 2008).

Once data for momentary affect at work has been collected, there are a range of analysis procedures that accommodate its multilevel and temporal nature (e.g., Bolger, Davis, & Rafaeli, 2003). We will not expand on these procedures here but it is worth pointing out that it is not just the level or intensity of affect that is of interest in analysing this sort of data, it is also its variability, its cycles (e.g., circadian or weekly), its responsiveness to work events and its rate of recovery from events (e.g., Beal & Ghandour, 2011).

Mood

In this section, we review the causes and consequences of mood at work. A schematic diagram of the main causes and consequences of mood at work is shown in Figure 1.

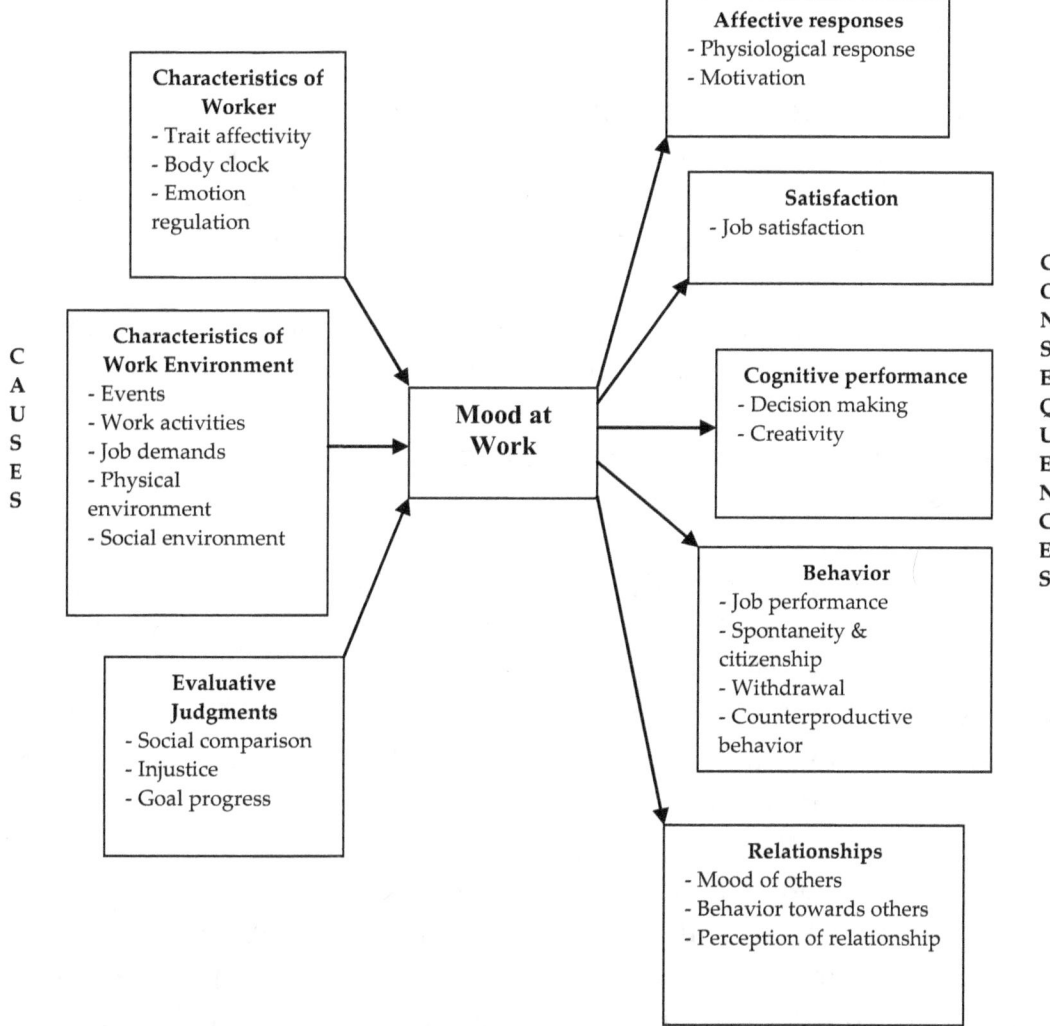

Figure 1. **Schematic diagram of the causes and consequences of momentary mood at work.**

Causes of Mood at Work

Research has devoted considerable attention to the consequences of affect, but according to Fisher (2008) "there has been almost no attention given to the real-time work setting causes of moods and emotions while working" (p.120). However, the research that has been conducted – including Fisher's own work – has established a range of sources for momentary mood in the workplace. We will differentiate these sources by grouping them into those that are located: in the worker, in the work environment, and in the workers' perceptions of their work environments or themselves.

Characteristics of the worker

Stable characteristics of individuals, such as their personal temperament, are strongly influenced by their genetic makeup and this makeup can thereby influence what they feel. For example, it has been estimated that genetic heritability may account for as much as half the variability in people's experienced happiness (Sheldon & Lyubomirsky, 2007). There may be two reasons for this: first, personal temperament can influence the events that individuals encounter because people are inclined to gravitate towards events that are congruent with their personality traits; and second, personal temperament can influence affective reactions to events because individuals are inclined to interpret events in a fashion that is congruent with their traits. In the workplace, it has been found that affective dispositions predict affective reactions. Specifically, it has been found that positive affectivity, which encapsulates a person's tendency to experience positive affect, is associated with more positive affective reactions while working, and likewise negative affectivity, which encapsulates a person's tendency to experience negative affect, is associated with more negative affective reactions while working (e.g., Fisher, 2002).

Characteristics of the individual contribute not only to the frequency and intensity of momentary affect but also to its variability across time. In particular, the combined influence of the individual's body clock and sleep-wake cycle produce circadian (daily) rhythms in activated mood (e.g., alertness) and pleasant mood (e.g., cheerfulness), although in the latter case the rhythm is sometimes masked unless specific circumstances prevail such as abnormal routines (e.g. shift work) or depression (e.g., Totterdell, 1995). For shift workers, alertness and cheerfulness are typically lower during the night, and the amount of time the worker spends on shift can lower them further (Totterdell, Spelten, Smith, Barton & Folkard, 1995). Workers on regular work schedules also exhibit diurnal cycles in mood (Stone, Smyth, Pickering & Schwartz, 1996; Weiss, Nicholas, & Daus, 1999) and longer mood cycles have also been found (e.g., weekly cycle; Stone, Hedges, Neale, & Satin, 1985), but these longer cycles appear to be determined more by external events than by physiological mechanisms.

The way in which workers use their personal resources can also influence their momentary affect. For example, teachers trained to use cognitive and behavioral engagement as affect regulation strategies were found to experience greater cheerfulness at work (Totterdell & Parkinson, 1999). Use of such resources may also diminish or exacerbate the impact of the work environment on mood. Hart, Wearing and Headey (1995), for example, found that emotion-focused coping exacerbated the negative impact of work experiences.

Characteristics of the work environment

Research on daily work stress has been influential in showing that daily events are as important to consider as major events when it comes to understanding what causes feelings at work. Kanner and colleagues' work on hassles and uplifts (Kanner Coyne, Schaefer, & Lazarus, 1981), for example, showed that the experience of persistent daily hassles (e.g., work overload, difficult colleagues/customers) produces negative feelings, while the experience of persistent daily uplifts (e.g., support, rewards) produces positive feelings.

According to AET (Weiss & Cropanzano, 1996), stable characteristics of the work environment make some events at work more likely than others and thereby influence how people feel at work. However, some characteristics are thought to promote events that cause positive feelings but do not influence negative feelings, while other characteristics promote events that cause negative feelings but do not influence positive feelings. The research evidence has largely supported this view. Events that are associated with interesting work, goal achievement, and rewarding interactions are more strongly associated with positive feelings, whereas daily stressors are more strongly associated with negative feelings (e.g., Basch & Fischer, 2000; Totterdell & Holman, 2003). Likewise, Fisher (2002) found that jobs with enriched characteristics, such as variety, task identity, significance, autonomy and feedback, produced more positive affective reactions, while jobs with greater role conflict produced more negative affective reactions.

The association between negative events and mood at work is typically stronger than the association between positive events and mood, but positive events are usually reported more frequently (e.g., Miner et al., 2005). In relation to the types of work environment characteristic that influence workers' affective reactions, it is possible to divide these into: 1) content of work activities, 2) job demands, 3) physical environment, and 4) social environment:

1) Work activities. The content of people's work task affects how they feel. Tasks that are repetitive, that offer low control, or that entail a too easy or a too difficult challenge produce negative feelings, whereas tasks that provide meaning and significance to people's work produce positive feelings (Fisher, 2008). For example, a recent experience sampling study by Glomb, Bhave, Miner, and Wall (2011) showed that employees felt more positive after they engaged in activities that involved doing good for others.

2) Job demands. Time sampling studies have identified a variety of job demands that produce negative moods when they are perceived to be high, including time pressure (Teuchmann, Totterdell, & Parker, 1999), workload (Repetti, 1993), overtime (Rau & Triemer, 2004), and role juggling (Williams, Suls, Alliger, Learner, & Wan, 1991). Studies have also shown that unpleasant mood arising from demands outside work can spillover into mood experienced while working (Williams & Alliger, 1994), and that recovery from work affects mood at work (Fritz, Sonnentag, Spector, & McInroe, 2010).

3) Physical environment. Brief and Weiss (2002) identified physical settings as a potential cause of moods and emotions at work but noted that research in this area was slim and had ignored obvious characteristics such as light and noise. This situation has marginally improved in subsequent years. For example, a study of work lighting by Kuller, Ballal, Laike, Mikellides, and Tonello (2006) found that mood was worse when indoor lighting was too bright or too dark, but this appeared to be due to perceived rather than objective illuminance.

4) Social environment. Interactions with other people at work are an influential cause of momentary affect (e.g., Repetti, 1993). An experience sampling study by Dimotakis, Scott and Koopman (2011) established that

interpersonal interactions have the same specificity of relationship with mood as other events, by showing that positive interpersonal interactions influence positive moods and negative interpersonal interactions influence negative moods.

Leaders or supervisors are a highly salient source of affect in the work social environment. One study found that workers reported fewer positive feelings when interacting with supervisors compared with interactions with co-workers and customers, unless their supervisors were transformational leaders in which case they reported feeling more positive throughout workdays (de Bono, Jackson, Foldes, Vinson, & Muros, 2007). This type of leader may produce more positive moods by providing more challenging task opportunities and positive feedback, or they may transmit their own positive moods to their followers through mood contagion (Bono & Ilies, 2006). Mood contagion appears to occur through a combination of reactive nonconscious processes and inferential conscious processes (van Kleef, 2009). In support of a mood contagion explanation, it has been shown experimentally that when leaders are unknowingly induced into particular moods they reproduce those moods in their followers (Sy, Côté, & Saavedra, 2005). Other studies have shown that mood linkage also occurs between team members (e.g., Ilies, Wegner, & Morgeson, 2007; Totterdell, 2000; Totterdell, Kellett,, Teuchmann, & Briner, 1998), so the mood of work colleagues is another source of mood.

Workers' evaluative judgments

When summarising research on the causes of mood at work, Brief and Weiss (2002) observed that "rarely did studies include objective indicators of those workplace features thought to produce moods and emotions" (p. 292). Some of the research described above suffers this same problem and may therefore have inadvertently captured workers' evaluative judgments as causes of mood rather than objective causes. For some researchers, however, workers' judgements or appraisals of their environment are the actual antecedents of mood, particularly if the mood is thought to arise from an interaction between the person and his or her environment rather than from one or the other.

A good example of this is found in research that concerns social comparison judgments. Using a diary study, Spence, Ferris, Brown and Heller (2011) showed that individuals experience lower levels of positive affect when they compare themselves to others who they perceive to be better off at work than themselves, whereas they experience higher levels of positive affect when they compare themselves to those who they consider worse off. Similarly, research on people's affective experience arising from different types of toxic event at work (such as bullying, insensitivity, and incompetence) suggests that what they have in common is people's perception of the injustice with which they are being treated (Lawrence, 2008). In a different line of work, control theories of affect (e.g., Carver & Scheier, 1990) suggest that affect arises from perceived progress towards goals. Few workplace studies have tested this idea but the basic tenets of control theory, if not the detail, have received empirical support (Alliger & Williams, 1993; Holman, Totterdell & Rogelberg, 2005; Zohar, 1999).

Consequences of Mood at Work

Empirical evidence shows that momentary mood at work has a range of potential consequences for workers. To review these consequences, we will group them into effects on workers': affective response, satisfaction, cognitive performance, behavior, and relationships. However, we begin by making a couple of general points about the effects of different types of mood. In the same way that positive and negative moods at work have different antecedents, they also usually have different effects (Ashkanasy & Humphrey, 2011). This may be due to their differential roles in guiding cognition and behavior. For example, Fredrickson's (2001) broaden and build theory suggests that momentary positive affect broadens people's thought-action repertoires and allows them to build their social and psychological resources. Negative mood, on the other hand, usually signals the presence of problems which leads to greater monitoring of the environment and corrective action (Forgas, 1995).

It has also been proposed that it is the relative balance of positive and negative affect – known as the positivity ratio – that determines whether people flourish or flounder in their environment (Fredrickson, 2013). In this framework, positive affect is hypothesised to undo the deleterious effects on mood of negative events (Fredrickson, Mancuso, Branigan, & Tugade, 2000).

Although, the positivity ratio has yet to be shown to be a better explanatory construct than its components, there is evidence to suggest that positive and negative affect should be considered in tandem because both are functional and the effects of one are dependent on the presence or absence of the other – this has been termed the dual tuning perspective (George, 2011). The consequences of momentary mood at work may also need to be considered with respect to a range of outcomes (rather than isolated indicators) and over longer time periods than those currently used. For example, the experience of frequent positive affect has been associated with various markers of life success (Lyubomirsky, King, & Diener, 2005).

Affective Response

Positive affect (PA) and negative affect (NA) may reflect the operation of different biological systems for engagement and inhibition that underlie approach and withdrawal behaviors (Watson, Wiese, Vaidya, & Tellegen, 1999). PA and NA would therefore be expected to relate differently to workers' physiological responses. In support of this, an experience sampling study by Ilies, Dimotakis and Watson (2010) showed that while PA and NA were both positively related to the heart rate of employees, only NA related to blood pressure (BP). Heart rate probably responds to the activating aspect of both PA and NA, whereas elevated BP is a distress response and so is likely to respond only to the negative signal of NA.

As well as affecting physiological responses, mood also influences workers' motivation to act (George & Brief, 1996; Kanfer & Stubblebine, 2008). Using a simulation task that required individuals to make daily financial investments, Seo, Bartunek, and Feldman Barrett (2010) found that investors expected to do better and sensed greater progress when they were in a pleasant mood and this made them less defensive, more effortful, and more persistent with a course of action; the investors also found larger rewards more attractive when they felt activated, and this increased their effort.

Satisfaction

Here we consider the effect of momentary mood on workers' evaluation of their job satisfaction. It should be noted that job satisfaction can have an affective as well as a cognitive component, which can lead to problems in separating cause from effect because affect may be present in both. For example, job satisfaction is often seen as an attitude that involves both an affective and a cognitive evaluation (see Brief & Weiss, 2002), but job satisfaction measures differ in the extent to which they involve each aspect (Fisher, 2000). Results in this area can also be affected depending on whether affect arising from the job or affect about the job is measured, or whether job satisfaction now or job satisfaction in general is measured (Judge & Kammeyer-Mueller, 2008; Wagner & Ilies, 2008).

Nevertheless, a number of experience sampling studies have shown that affective reactions predict job satisfaction (e.g., Dimotakis et al., 2011; Judge & Ilies, 2004, Weiss et al.,1999), thus supporting the hypothesized relationship between affect and satisfaction proposed in AET. However, this relationship is not always found (e.g. Fisher, 2002) and can also go in the reverse direction from satisfaction to affect (Judge & Ilies, 2004). The effect of mood on job satisfaction appears to be short-lived, but Fuller et al. (2003) did find a relationship between daily mood and job satisfaction the next day. Dimotakis et al. (2011) found that positive and negative affect had an interactive effect on job satisfaction such that positive affect weakened the association between negative affect and low job satisfaction, which supports the undoing hypothesis (Fredrickson et al., 2000) and the dual tuning perspective (George, 2011).

Cognitive performance

 The findings for job satisfaction illustrate that mood can affect people's judgments. Mood can also bias other judgements and thereby affect performance. One aspect of performance at work is decision-making and a number of studies have found that when managers are in positive moods they are likely to be more optimistic and take greater risks (see Ashkanasy & Humphrey, 2011). Mittal and Ross (1998), for example, found that decision-makers faced with uncertainty were more willing to take a risk when they were in a positive mood than a negative mood. There is some support for the happier-and-smarter hypothesis as opposed to the sadder-but-wiser hypothesis (Staw & Barsade, 1993), but intense positive affect can reduce decision quality by increasing reliance on use of cognitive heuristics (Ng & Wong, 2008). For intuitive decision-making, it appears to be intensity of affect rather than valence that promotes it (Sinclair, Ashkanasy, &

Chattopadhyay, 2010). Moods can also influence group decision-making. For example, Van Knippenberg, Kooij-de Bode, and van Ginkel (2010) found that groups in positive moods made worse decisions, but only if they were low in trait negative affect.

Another aspect of cognitive performance is creativity. Positive mood is thought to facilitate flexible cognition and divergent thinking which appears to aids tasks that require creativity at work (Amabile, Barsade, Mueller, & Staw, 2005; Madjar, Oldham, & Pratt, 2002). Using a diary study, Binnewies and Wörnlein (2011) showed that positive affect at the start of a day in a group of architects was positively related to their creativity that day. The same study found that negative affect was negatively related to creativity but only if the architects had low control over their job. Other research, however, has found that negative moods predict more creative performance, especially if creativity is required and rewarded in the job (George & Zhou, 2002). Eisenberg and James (2005) have suggested that inconsistent findings in this area have been due to failure to take into account a number of additional influencing factors such as duration of effect and task type. Creativity in organizations is also sometimes only the first part of a longer process of innovation that requires additional behaviors to translate ideas into practice. In a review of the impact of affect on innovation, Rank and Frese (2008) concluded that positive affect facilitates innovation, as does negative affect under some circumstances such as when it involves high arousal. In the next section we consider the effects of mood on some other sorts of behavior.

Behavior

Probably the most obvious job behavior in the workplace to consider is that of task performance. Employees who experience more positive moods have been shown to receive higher ratings of their job performance (Staw, Sutton & Pelled, 1994), but there have been surprisingly few studies of the relationship between momentary mood and task performance (Judge & Kammeyer-Mueller, 2008). A study of professional sports performance showed positive relations between positive moods and both subjective and objective performance, but also showed that for some types of mood (e.g. anxiety) the relationship can be positive or negative depending on the person (Totterdell, 1999, 2000). Miner and Glomb (2010) found that call centre employees handled customer calls more quickly when they were in positive moods, but this did not affect customer ratings of service quality.

The relationship between momentary mood and job performance is not always straightforward. For example, the importance of examining the relationship over extended timeframes was illustrated in a diary study conducted by Richard and Diefendorff (2011). Focusing on a single performance episode (exam preparation), they discovered that although positive mood was related to increased performance goals on the same day, it also related to reduced performance effort the next day. Positive mood may therefore increase expectancy but also reduce a person's current concerns about progress. The relationship between mood and performance can also be moderated by other affect-related variables, including attention to mood (Miner & Glomb, 2010) mood regulation (Brown, Westbrook, & Challagalla, 2005), and emotion regulatory resource (Janssen, Lam, & Huang, 2010).

There are a number of work behaviors, both positive and negative, that lie outside of task performance. These include discretionary behaviors that involve engagement with the workplace such as citizenship, and others that involve withdrawal from the workplace such as deviance. Positive mood has been associated with a number of positive behaviors at work, including organizational spontaneity (George, 1991; George & Brief, 1992) and organizational citizenship (Ilies, Scott, & Judge, 2006; Miner et al., 2005; Spence et al., 2007). Positive mood has also been associated with less withdrawal behavior including absenteeism (George, 1989) and task avoidance (Miner et al., 2005). However, this can be complicated by the fact that workers may use withdrawal behavior to repair moods and so positive mood can be positively associated with withdrawal depending on when it is measured (Miner & Glomb, 2010). Several studies have found that negative moods, such as anxiety, are associated with counterproductive work behaviors such as aggression and sabotage (see Ashkanasy & Humphrey, 2011), but discrete emotions such as anger appear to offer greater explanatory value for these behaviors (see Penney & Spector, 2008).

Relationships

Earlier, when considering the causes of momentary mood, we mentioned how leaders and colleagues have been found to influence workers' moods via the process of mood contagion. Influencing other people's mood via mood contagion can be seen as a consequence as well as a cause of mood. This influence occurs in part through expression of affect, which can be seen as a proximal consequence of experienced affect, and has been shown to influence the feelings and service quality ratings of customers (Pugh, 2001).

Momentary mood in workers can also affect their behavior towards others. George (1991), for example, found that sales staff engaged in more prosocial behavior when they were in positive mood states (but not traits), and that when they directed this behavior at customers (e.g., by helping them) it was associated with enhanced job performance and satisfaction. Mood may also influence how people negotiate with others in organizations. Positive mood appears to encourage greater cooperation, but the research evidence is slender and has tended to focus on discrete emotions (Brief & Weiss, 2002).

As well as influencing how other people feel and influencing behavior towards others, a third way in which moods at work can influence relationships is through changing perceptions of those relationships. For example, Barsky, Kaplan and Beal (2011) have outlined various processes by which moods and emotions can influence the fairness judgments that people make at work. These judgments usually concern how employees feel they are being treated by others in the organization or by the organization itself. Effects on relationships also extend beyond the organization. In a recent review of the role of affect in the interface between work and the family, Eby, Maher, and Butts (2010) concluded that negative mood states at work are usually associated with greater work-family conflict. The studies they considered found gender differences in how the conflict manifests itself, but these effects were complex. The effects of workers' mood states also appear to spillover to their children, as well as to their partners, but research is sparse in this area.

Discrete Emotions

In this section of the review, we discuss the causes and consequences of discrete emotions within the workplace. We then turn the spotlight on two discrete emotions that are particularly relevant to everyday organizational life and consider what prompts these emotions and what effects they have at work. Figure 2 illustrates the main proposed causes and consequences of discrete emotions.

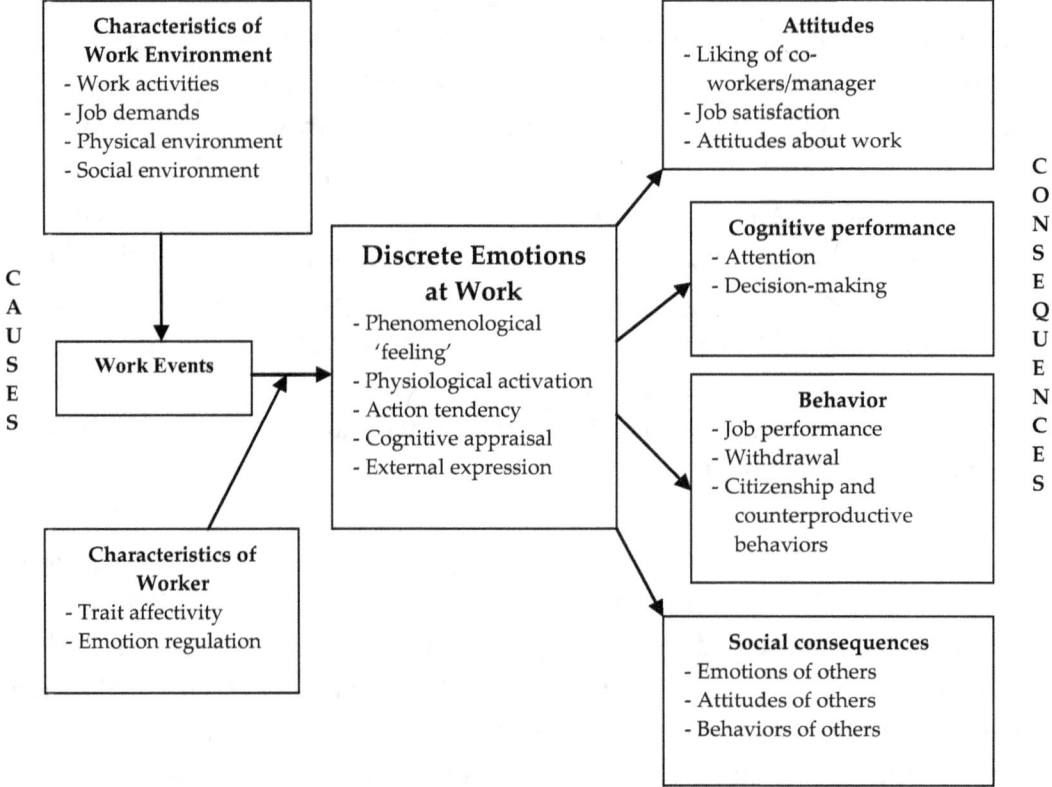

Figure 2. **Schematic diagram of the causes and consequences of discrete emotions at work.**

Causes of Discrete Emotions

As suggested earlier, discrete emotions differ from moods in three main ways. First, they tend to be shorter lasting. Second, they are usually more intense. Third, they are directed at specific objects or events; in other words, emotions are *about* something. It is this third characteristic that is most salient when it comes to considering the causes of discrete emotions. While moods may be precipitated by more stable features of the work environment or the employee's characteristics, discrete emotions are invariably triggered by specific work events.

How do events in the workplace produce a discrete emotional response? Appraisal theories of emotion, originating with Arnold (1960), explain that people evaluate the events they experience in an appraisal process that serves to relate events to people and their goals, and it is the appraisal of events that prompts emotions. Most researchers seem to agree that appraisals are a two-stage process (Zajonc, 1980). The first stage occurs immediately upon encountering an emotive event and takes the form of a reflex-like automatic sense of whether the event is harmful or beneficial. This appraisal motivates a broad approach (pleasant) or avoidance (unpleasant) feeling. The second stage of appraisal swiftly follows and it is this stage that determines the specific 'color' of the emotional experience. Secondary appraisals are more conscious and more complex in nature and take into account causal attributions, the nature of the event, future consequences of the event, potential for responding to the event, and so on.

Workplace events may be appraised differently by different people and so may elicit contrasting discrete emotions. For example, while one person might evaluate an upcoming deadline as a threat, and so experience a negative emotion, another person might view the same deadline as a challenge, and so experience a positive emotion. Similarly, different workplace events might elicit the same emotions; a person might be angered as a result of being yelled at by a coworker and also as a result of a computer failure. However, according to Lazarus (1991), the appraisal that underlies different people's experience of a particular emotion will be the same. Specifically, each discrete emotion is thought to be associated with a different 'core relational theme' (i.e., a distinctive secondary appraisal) and these themes can help us to understand the causes of discrete emotions. In Table 1, we highlight the core relational themes of some of the discrete emotions that are most commonly-experienced at work, and suggest example events that might prompt such appraisals.

Table 1. Causes of discrete emotions

Discrete emotion	Core relational theme	Example causal events
Happiness	Making good progress towards realization of a goal	Finishing a piece of work on time
Pride	Enhancement of one's ego-identity by taking credit for a valued object or achievement	Winning an award
Hope	Fearing the worst but yearning for the best	Applying for a new job
Relief	A distressing goal-incongruent condition that has changed for the better or gone away	Having a deadline extended for an important piece of work
Gratitude	Recognition or appreciation of an altruistic gift	A coworker helping with one's work
Sadness	Having experienced an irrevocable loss	A close friend leaving the organization
Anxiety	Facing an uncertain, existential threat	Announcement of potential job losses
Anger	A demeaning offense against me and mine	A customer being rude and impertinent
Guilt	Having transgressed a moral imperative	Taking credit for a coworker's idea
Envy	Wanting what someone else has	A coworker getting promoted
Shame	Having failed to live up to an ego-ideal	Submitting a below-standard piece of work

Note. Core relational themes are from Lazarus (1991) and Lazarus and Lazarus (1994)

Although different events may elicit the same emotion, some attempts have been made to classify the types of events that are most likely to elicit particular emotions in the workplace. Basch and Fisher (2000) surveyed a sample of hotel workers and reported, for example, that pride was most commonly-prompted by receiving recognition, pleasure usually followed goal achievement, anger was most often precipitated by acts of co-workers, and embarrassment stemmed from making mistakes. More broadly, workplace events that involve interactions with other people, notably one's manager, seem to be the most likely to elicit an emotional response (Basch & Fisher, 2000; Dasborough, 2006).

Researchers have also identified some *aspects* of workplace events that reliably influence how emotions are experienced by employees. In particular, and in line with appraisal theories (e.g., Lazarus, 1991), events that are more salient to people and their goals tend to produce more intense and also longer-lasting emotions (e.g., Verduyn, Delvauz, Van Coillie, Tuerlinckx, & Van Mechelen, 2009). Research from a variety of domains converges to suggest that negative events are usually more salient than positive events, perhaps because this is advantageous in an evolutionary sense (i.e., paying more attention to threats in the environment is more adaptive for survival) (Baumeister, Bratslavsky, Finkenauer, & Vohs, 2001; Rozin & Royzman, 2001); thus negative workplace events may produce more intense and longer-lasting emotions compared with positive events.

Earlier, we suggested that discrete emotions are caused by proximate work events whereas moods are more influenced by aspects of the work environment or the employee's characteristics. However, AET (Weiss & Cropanzano, 1996) contends that the more stable features that influence moods may also affect discrete emotions. Features of the work environment, like work activities, job demands, and the physical and social environment, all influence the likelihood of events occurring at work. For instance, a job in which the majority of work activities involve dealing with customers increases the chances of having negative customer interactions. Likewise, a job with high demands increases the chances of having tight deadlines.

Employees' characteristics also influence the ways in which workplace events are appraised and thus the emotions they elicit. In their recent review, Kuppens and Tong (2010) discuss how appraisals are by nature subjective and therefore prone to individual differences, and suggest that personal temperament may be linked to systematic patterns regarding how events are appraised. For example, people high in optimism tend to appraise events positively while people high in pessimism tend to appraise events negatively (Scheier & Carver, 1985), and those high in self-efficacy are more likely to appraise events as something they can cope with compared with those low in self-efficacy (Bandura, 1977). Similarly, temperament may influence how salient events are to employees and thus the intensity of the emotional reactions they experience; those who are high in trait neuroticism have a lower threshold for reacting to events and so experience more intense and variable emotions (Eysenck, 1967). In addition, employees may choose to deliberately influence the ways in which they appraise events in order to control the emotions they experience. Reappraisal involves viewing an event in a different light (e.g., by viewing the event from another perspective) in order to produce a desired emotional response (Gross, 1998), and is one of the most-commonly used forms of emotion regulation in the workplace as it is both an effective coping strategy and a way for employees, particularly those in service occupations, to produce the emotions that are considered appropriate for them to display (Grandey, 2000).

Consequences of Discrete Emotions

Discrete emotions, like moods, are affective feeling states. As such, they have similar consequences for employees' satisfaction, decision-making, creativity, performance, and relationships, as reviewed earlier in this article. However, there is more to discrete emotions than just an internal 'feeling'. Most researchers agree that discrete emotions are associated with a particular pattern of physiology, action tendencies (i.e., actions that the person is primed towards), cognitions, and expressions, as well as a distinctive phenomenological experience (Briner, 1999; Parkinson, 1995). For example, the emotion of anger is associated with increased heart rate and perspiration, the action tendency of aggression, cognitions associated with other-directed blame, and expressions including a clenched jaw, flared nostrils, a fixated stare, a squared-off stance, and loud and aggressive speech and vocalizations. These components of discrete emotion are thought to represent an organized and cohesive set of responses that serve an adaptive function in terms of survival (Darwin, 1872), but as we discuss below, each different component may have downstream consequences for employees in their everyday work lives that may be functional in some cases but dysfunctional in others.

When an emotional stimulus is encountered in the environment, a set of short-term physiological responses are apparent (Zajonc, 1980). There is some disagreement as to whether each discrete emotion is associated with a distinct pattern of physiological changes (see Mauss & Robinson, 2009, for a review), but most agree that: i) emotions are associated with activation of the autonomic nervous system (ANS), which can manifest in terms of increases in skin conductance response, heart rate and heart rate variability, cardiac output, and blood pressure, and ii) more intense and higher arousal emotions (e.g., rage, fear) are associated with higher ANS activation. There also seems to be a distinction between positive and negative emotions in terms of the responses they elicit, with negative states typically associated with greater activation compared with positive states (Cacioppo, Berntson, Larsen, Poehlmann, & Ito, 2000). The physiological component of discrete emotions has received little direct research attention with respect to how it might influence work-related consequences, yet it seems likely that physiological changes associated with emotions will have implications for employees (Elfenbein, 2007). In particular, ANS activation may have implications for work with respect to performance; the classic Yerkes-Dodson (1908) inverted-U law predicts that performance will be optimal at intermediate levels of arousal and poorer at both low and high levels of arousal, because at high levels attention becomes restricted and task-relevant cues may be ignored whereas at low levels the individual is not motivated for action. This implies that activation from emotions could have a beneficial impact on work performance, but at too high levels (e.g., when experiencing extremely intense negative emotions like rage), performance decrements may be experienced. In support of this assertion, research on violence at work suggests that those who are exposed to incidents of violence (an 'affective event' likely to elicit intense negative emotion) experience poorer concentration and diverted attention (e.g., intrusive thoughts) and consequently report poorer work performance (Coles, Koritsas, Boyle, & Stanley, 2007).

The action tendency component of emotion refers to the automatic impulse for action that accompanies the internal feeling of emotion (Frijda, 2010). Action tendencies activate and prioritize patterns of behavior that relate to the core relational themes of the discrete emotion being experienced (Lazarus, 1991), and are thus likely to influence employees' behaviors while at work. Broadly speaking, negative emotions motivate behaviors that aim to change and rectify a situation (e.g., negative emotions are associated with higher intentions to turnover; Grandey, Tam, & Brauburger, 2002), whereas positive emotions motivate behaviors that maintain the status quo (e.g., helping and organizational citizenship behaviors that maintain positive affect; Spector & Fox, 2002). However, discrete emotions do not map perfectly to particular behaviors; they increase the *likelihood* of particular patterns of actions (Frijda, 2010), but although we sometimes act strictly on impulse, more often we choose our behavior taking into account factors relating to the situation in which the emotion is experienced (Feldman Barrett, 2006). In the workplace in particular, there are many situational constraints that influence the behaviors that are selected, particularly for lower status employees (Fitness, 2000). For example, when a high status worker feels angry because he or she was overlooked for a promotion, the worker might confront his or her manager, whereas in the same situation a low status worker might elect to withdraw and silently seethe.

The cognitive component of discrete emotions similarly has important consequences for employees' cognitions and behaviors at work. Cognitive appraisals provide information to people about how events and objects in their environment relate to them and their goals (Lazarus, 1991). This not only produces the phenomenological experience of emotion but can also influence people's attitudes towards the events and objects that are the subject of the appraisal (Schwarz & Clore, 1983). For example, when a coworker helps an employee to finish some work in time for a deadline, the employee might appraise this as a positive event that the coworker is responsible for, in turn eliciting both the feeling of gratitude *and* a positive attitude (e.g., liking) towards the coworker. Appraisals and the attitudes they influence may also affect workers' interpersonal behaviors (e.g., in the above scenario, the employee might reciprocate the coworker's help in a future interaction) (Weiss & Cropanzano, 1996). Research tells us that we often misattribute feelings and attitudes (Schwarz & Clore, 1983), and this might help to explain why specific work events might give rise to attitudes and behaviors concerning 'work' or one's job more broadly (e.g., disliking one's job as a result of a conflict interaction with a customer). Because appraisals focus employees' attention on a particular issue, they can help workers to solve problems relating to the appraised event and can facilitate decision-making processes (Damasio, 1994). Conversely, the cognitive capacity taken up by attention to the appraised event can impede performance on tasks that are cognitively complex (Beal, Weiss, Barros, & MacDermid, 2005), especially in the case of negative appraisals as these are considered more salient and so demand more attention (Motowildo, Packard, & Manning, 1986). Specific discrete emotions may also have distinctive effects in terms of the information processing styles they prompt; anger, for example, is thought to lead to more heuristic processing (Bodenhausen, Sheppard, & Kramer, 1994), which can be useful when facing a simple task that must be performed quickly, yet maladaptive when facing an intricate task that requires attention to detail.

Finally, the expressive component of discrete emotions is likely to have important work-related consequences with respect to coordinating social interactions in the workplace. Perhaps the most obvious way in which emotions are expressed is facially; each discrete emotion is thought to be associated with a pattern of involuntary facial muscle actions that produces a distinctive facial expression (e.g., an upturn of the outer corners of the lips and wrinkling around the eyes for happiness) (Ekman, 1972). Aside from facial expressions, discrete emotions may be associated with a number of other forms of expression, including gestures, posture, touch, vocalizations, and tone and pitch of speech (Sauter, 2010). An employee's outward expression of a discrete emotion, via the face, body, and voice, is likely to transmit his or her felt state to others in his or her environment (e.g., coworkers, customers) as a result of unconscious primitive contagion mechanisms as well as more conscious appraisals of the employee's attitudes and goals (Van Kleef, 2009). Thus, employees' emotions may have consequences for the feelings of others they come into contact with. Strong evidence for this contagion effect has been found in workplace studies, particularly between employees and their customers during service encounters (Barger & Grandey, 2006; Pugh, 2001). Expressed emotion may also function to regulate social interactions by communicating information to others about how we would like them to engage with us. According to Parkinson's (1996) theory, the core relational appraisal themes of each discrete emotion can actually be seen as core communicative messages. For example, guilt, which is associated with the appraisal of 'having transgressed a moral imperative', communicates that one would like to be forgiven. Similarly, an employee's expression of pride signals to coworkers that the employee would like his or her achievement to be recognized. These messages, in turn, are likely to influence the emotions and interaction behaviors of others in the workplace, as demonstrated by Van Kleef and colleagues who show that in negotiation situations, the emotions expressed by negotiators strongly influenced the concession behavior of their opponents (e.g., Van Kleef, De Dreu, & Manstead, 2004).

Research On Specific Discrete Emotions

In this section, we focus on two discrete emotions that are especially salient to everyday work life: anger and envy.

Anger

Anger has been defined by Gibson and Callister (2010) as "an emotion that involves an appraisal of responsibility for wrongdoing by another person or entity and often includes the goal of correcting the perceived wrong" (p. 68). Phenomenologically, anger is a high arousal unpleasant and aversive state. It can be experienced at varying levels of intensity, ranging from low-level irritation to full-blown rage. The physiological components of anger are often described as part of the anger experience (e.g., feeling one's heart racing and one's fists tightening as blood flow to the hands increases).

With respect to the causes of anger at work, anger has been described as a social emotion, in that the events that precipitate anger tend to directly concern the actions of another person (Averill, 1982). Gibson and Callister (2010) expand on this understanding by proposing three key types of interpersonal events that typically cause employees to feel angry: i) events that are perceived to be unjust; ii) events that interfere with or frustrate one's goal attainment; and iii) events involving interpersonal conflict. Injustice in particular is thought to be the main cause of workplace anger and, in line with this, studies by Domagalski and Steelman (2005) and Fitness (2000) report unjust treatment to be the most common trigger for anger at work. The source of injustice may vary depending on the type of occupation the employee works within; for many one's supervisor is seen as the main source of injustice (e.g., Fitness, 2000), but within service work anger may be more often elicited as a result of injustice from customers (Grandey et al., 2002). Differences may also be apparent based on status. For example, in Fitness's (2000) study, for supervisors anger was mainly elicited as a result of others' job incompetence (an event likely to interfere with the supervisor's goal attainment), whereas for subordinates being treated unjustly and being humiliated were prime causes.

As stated earlier, discrete emotions may have both functional and dysfunctional consequences, and anger is no exception. Positive consequences of anger include signaling to the person who is experiencing the anger that his or her goals are being blocked (Frijda, 1986), triggering "a bias towards seeing the self as powerful and capable" (Lerner & Tiedens, 2006, p. 125), and communicating to others when they have wronged a person (Parkinson, 1996), thus enabling the person and the target of anger to deal with the offending situation. In support of these positive consequences, Bies (1987) argues that anger is considered vital to motivate people to address issues of injustice and inequity at work, while Tafrate, Kassinove, and Dundin (2002) report that around half of the time expressions of anger lead to positive consequences for interpersonal relationships. Within specific situations, anger may also be advantageous for work performance. For instance, within the context of negotiations, expressing anger is thought to evoke emotions in others that can help the negotiator (e.g., eliciting fear; Keltner & Kring, 1998), in turn leading to more opponent concessions (Van Kleef et al., 2004).

Conversely, anger may also have negative consequences. Negative health consequences include raised blood pressure and increased chance of developing heart disease (Begley, 1994). Other negative consequences for angry workers include negative changes to others' perceptions (e.g., in Glomb & Hulin's, 1997, study of supervisor-subordinate interactions, supervisors who expressed anger were rated lower by observers compared with those who did not express anger; likewise, in Lewis's, 2000, study of leaders, anger expressions reduced subordinates' perceptions of leadership effectiveness) and reciprocal anger responses towards the employee (Friedman et al., 2004). Damage to interpersonal relationships can also follow from anger displays; Allred, Mallozzi, Matsui, and Raia (1997) demonstrated that negotiators who expressed higher anger had less desire to work with each other in the future and achieved fewer joint gains. In addition to these consequences for angry employees, anger is associated with negative interpersonal behaviors that can be damaging for other people and the workplace more widely. These forms of incivility and aggression are often directed towards the person perceived to be source of anger (i.e., revenge behaviors) but sometimes displaced to others or to the organization more generally, ultimately creating a more harmful organizational climate (Andersson & Pearson, 1999; Bies & Tripp, 1998; Fox & Spector, 1999).

So when is anger functional and when is it dysfunctional? A number of factors have been proposed to influence the consequences of anger in the workplace. Gender is one such factor; for example, Gibson, Schweitzer, Callister, and Gray (2009) reported that anger expressions by women are received less favorably than equivalent expressions by men. Status may also influence how anger is received by others; according to Fitness (2000), supervisors are more likely than subordinates to think that anger incidents have been successfully resolved, while Van Kleef, De Dreu, Pietroni, and Manstead, (2006) demonstrated that negotiators only conceded more to angry opponents of a higher status than them. Another important factor that is likely to influence the effects of anger within organizations is the intensity of the anger expression. Studies by Gibson et al. (2009) and Glomb (2002) suggests that anger expressions of lower intensity are associated with more functional consequences whereas anger expressions of higher intensity are associated with more negative consequences, including lower job satisfaction and performance and higher stress. Geddes and Callister's (2007) dual threshold model explains these differences, suggesting that expressing anger at a relatively low intensity is functional as it motivates people to resolve the anger-provoking situation rather than allowing a problem or issue to continue. However, expressing anger at too high an intensity is dysfunctional as this is construed as a deviation from normal and acceptable behavior, meaning that the person who expressed the anger is then seen as a problem and so the anger-provoking situation is unlikely to be resolved.

With respect to consequences for performance, the type of task is another factor that will help to determine the effects of anger. According to Miron-Spektor and Rafaeli's (2009) theoretical model, anger restricts cognitive processing, which is advantageous for simple tasks that benefit from narrowed attention but impedes performance in complex cognitive tasks, for instance those involving creativity. In support of this assertion, a study by De Dreu, Giebels, and Van de Vliert (1998) showed that when opponents exchanged threats during negotiation, leading to increased anger, this inhibited the negotiators' creativity and flexibility of thinking, ultimately resulting in less integrative agreements. A recent study on the interpersonal effects of anger further showed that the performance consequences of being subjected to someone else's anger similarly depended on the task type; in a customer service simulation study, listening to an angry customer facilitated participants' performance in solving analytic problems but impeded performance in solving creative problems (Miron-Spektor, Efrat-Treister, Rafaeli, & Schwartz-Cohen, 2011).

Envy

We now turn our attention to considering a second discrete emotion: envy. Envy is an aversive, negative emotion, defined by Vecchio (2000) as "a pattern of thoughts, emotions, and behaviors that results from an employee's loss of self-esteem in response to a referent other's obtainment of outcomes that one strongly desires" (p. 162). The term envy is often used interchangeably with the term for another discrete emotion, jealousy, which is characterized by a fear of losing something good to someone else (Smith, Kim, & Parrott, 1988). Envy and jealousy share many similarities, as both emotions involve social comparison with another person or persons and the phenomenological experience of diminished self-worth and inferiority resulting from this process (Ambrose, Harland, & Kulik, 1991). The key difference is that envy does not involve direct competition with a rival; one can be envious of something someone else has even though the other person's gain is not necessarily at one's own expense and, because of this, jealousy is thought to be somewhat more socially acceptable or *understandable* within organizations compared with envy (Vecchio, 2000). Although research on envy has mostly focused on envy within romantic relationships, in recent years research on envy in the workplace has emerged as an important topic, with evidence suggesting that envy is a widespread emotion at work (Miner, 1990; Vecchio, 1995).

In terms of the causes of envy at work, the primary cause of envy is social comparison; thus envy can arise any time an employee compares himself or herself unfavorably with someone else (Dunn & Schweitzer, 2006). Such comparisons are likely to be especially common in organizations that have limited resources (e.g., limited promotions, bonuses) or in highly competitive environments (Vecchio, 1995). Dunn and Schweitzer (2006) further suggest that because supervisors make important decisions about resource allocation, they may play an important role in prompting envy, particularly if such decisions are judged to be unfair.

Like anger, envy may have positive and negative consequences. On the positive side, envy seems to boost people's attention to information about others and thus facilitate recall. Hill, DelPriore, and Vaughan (2011) demonstrate this across a series of priming studies and argue that the effects of envy on cognitive processes are evolutionarily adaptive, in that paying greater attention to aspects of an envied person's life can help people to determine ways in which they themselves can achieve the same outcomes. Another positive consequence of envy may be motivation towards self-improvement. Because envy highlights a discrepancy between what another has and what one currently has, it can provide a motivating force (Tesser, 1991). In line with this suggestion, research has reported links between envy and employees' behaviors intended to improve their position within their organization (Cohen-Charash, 2009), as well as links between feelings of envy and improved job performance (Schaubroeck & Lam, 2004). In a recent series of studies, Van de Ven, Zeelenberg, and Pieters (2011) similarly provide evidence that feeling envious motivates people to study harder and predicts improved performance in tasks relating to intelligence and creativity.

On the negative side, employees' experiences of envy may lead to generalized feelings of anxiety and depression (Cohen-Charash, 2009) as well as dissatisfaction with their work (Vecchio, 2005) and intention to quit (Vecchio, 1995; 2000). Envy may also have cognitive costs; paying greater attention to envied others may require valued self-regulatory resources and therefore cause fatigue and reduced task performance (Hill et al., 2011). While envy does not often have interpersonal effects via its expressive component, because people usually try to conceal their envy, it may have extreme negative consequences in terms of how the envious person acts towards others. In particular, because envy concerns a desire for what someone else has, it can be associated with feelings of hostility towards the envied other (Cohen-Charash, 2009) and behaviors intended to remove or destroy the envied other's advantage (Dunn & Schweitzer, 2006). For example, studies have reported links between workplace envy and behaviors aimed to harm envied employees' reputation and performance, such as backstabbing, spreading malicious gossip, and providing misinformation (Vecchio, 1995). Employees experiencing envy may even be willing to sacrifice their own outcomes in the pursuit of diminishing the envied other's relative advantage (Parks, Rumble, & Posey, 2002).

Because the negative consequences of being envied are apparent (e.g., in terms of envious others engaging in harmful behaviors towards oneself), employees may fear being the target of envy, which in turn might influence their behavior. For instance, studies have linked fear of being the target of envy with employees downplaying their achievements or self-handicapping to avoid too much success (Natale, Campana, & Sora, 1988). On a more positive note, studies have also reported that fear of envy may lead to more prosocial helping behavior to protect against potential negative interpersonal feelings (Van de Ven, Zeelenberg, & Pieters, 2010).

A key factor that might help to explain when envy leads to positive consequences and when it has more dysfunctional outcomes is the type of envy that is experienced. Van de Ven, Zeelenberg, and Pieters (2009) distinguish two types of envy, which they refer to as benign envy and malicious envy. These types of envy are most easily differentiated by the action tendencies they are associated with; while benign envy focuses on wishing you had what someone else has and therefore motivates people to improve themselves, malicious envy focuses on wishing the other person did not have what you want and so motivates people to destroy the envied other. Thus, benign envy can convey benefits for people's work motivation and performance (e.g., Van de Ven et al., 2011), whereas malicious envy does not have the same benefits and instead drives feelings of hostility, ill-will, and negative interpersonal behaviors (e.g., Vecchio, 1995).

Summary

Moods and discrete emotions are part and parcel of work life. Research in the past two decades has begun to get to grips with understanding the multiple causes and multiple consequences of these different types of momentary affect at work. Affective events theory has proven useful in guiding this venture and looks set to be both complemented and challenged by other theories. Studying momentary affect is not an easy undertaking because of its transitory and dynamic nature but it has been helped by the emergence of various time-sampling methods that enable moods and emotions to be studied in real-time in work settings. Much of the research to date has focused on differences in the causes and consequences of positive and negative affect states. In general, positive affect states have been associated with more positive outcomes, but that is not always the case and the effects are sometimes dependent on the presence of other factors. Empirical evidence in many areas is still sparse and there are many remaining research challenges, some of which we present next.

Future Research Directions

Here we present some key questions that future research on momentary affect at work will need to address. Each of these questions encapsulates a different kind of challenge. The challenges and questions are summarised in Table 2.

Table 2. Summary of ten challenges for future research on momentary affect at work

Future Research Challenge	Research Question
1. Theory challenge	What is the role of anticipated emotion in driving behavior at work?
2. Design challenge	How can research be designed so that it reflects the temporal nature of the affective experience being investigated?
3. Process challenge	How and why do individuals differ in their response to events and in their recovery from them?
4. Conceptual challenge	What is the conceptual status of affect-related constructs such as engagement and flow – are they forms of affect, motivation, or attitude?
5. Research deficit challenge	How can the study of discrete emotions be facilitated and integrated with research on moods?
6. New topic challenge	What are the interpersonal causes and consequences of momentary affect at work?
7. Measurement challenge	How can different types of affect measurement be integrated?
8. Analytic challenge	What analytic procedures are best suited to investigating temporal dynamics in affect?
9. Intervention challenge	What interventions are effective in enhancing momentary affect at work?
10. Sustainability challenge	Can changes in momentary affect at work be sustained in the long-term?

Future Research Questions

1) What is the role of anticipated emotion in driving behavior at work (*theory challenge*)?

According to affective events theory (Weiss & Cropanzano, 1996), feelings directly drive behavior at work, but according to feedback theory (Baumeister et al., 2007) it is more common for behaviors to pursue anticipated emotions. Feedback theory implies that workers do not just respond to events, they also shape how they feel through processes involving imagination, behavioral feedback, and emotion-based learning. Although there is some empirical research on this topic (e.g., anticipated regret) in other contexts, this alternative conception needs articulating and testing in the context of work settings.

2) How can research be designed so that it reflects the temporal nature of the affective experience being investigated (*design challenge*)?

More careful consideration of the temporal characteristics and temporal experience of affect is needed in the design of future research because researchers do not at present have a good grasp of whether the time intervals in their designs are appropriate (Harter, Schmidt, Asplund, Killham, & Agrawal, 2010). Experience sampling studies suggest that many emotions have a short life span (< 2 hr) unless reinstated (Verduyn et al., 2009) so some designs may miss them. Current research design also pays insufficient attention to: the amount of time required for the causes of emotions and moods to have their effect, how long emotion and mood effects last, and whether emotion and mood effects are different at different times of day or week. Understanding how individuals convert their continuous temporal experience of work into meaningful affective episodes will also form part of this challenge (Beal & Weiss, 2013).

3) How and why do individuals differ in their response to events and in their recovery from them (*process challenge*)?

Research has established that individuals have a set-point or equilibrium level for affect valence that is usually mildly positive (see Parkinson, Totterdell, Briner & Reynolds, 1996). Events at work deflect individuals from this baseline, but individuals differ in their sensitivity to events and may also return to their baseline at different rates (Bowling, Beehr, Wagner, Libkuman, 2005). How and why these parameters vary is not well understood, although differences in affect regulation ability may be part of the explanation (e.g., Totterdell & Parkinson, 1999).

4) What is the conceptual status of affect-related constructs such as engagement and flow – are they forms of affect, motivation, or attitude (*conceptual challenge*)?

There is currently considerable interest within organizational research in constructs that appear to have an affective component, but that also have motivational and attitudinal components. For example, state work engagement has been described as a work attitude, but it is also thought to be part of the higher-order construct of happiness (Fisher, 2010; Harter et al, 2010). The conceptual status of these constructs needs to be clear, because the causes, processes and consequences of affect and attitudes are not the same.

5) How can the study of discrete emotions be facilitated and integrated with research on moods (*research deficit challenge*)?

Gooty, Gavin, and Ashkanasy (2009) found that less than 10 per cent of research on emotion published in leading management journals has been based on field tests of discrete emotions. As Gross (2010) observed, "catching emotions as they unfold is a bit like catching butterflies, only harder" (p. 213), which may discourage researchers from venturing into the field to catch them. Researchers may also be discouraged by gauging that their research will be too narrow if they focus on one discrete emotion and not others. It is difficult to identify communality across the emotions when they are studied in isolation. Part of the answer may lie in collective ventures that allow researchers to pool their findings (e.g. special sections of journals, conference symposia). It may also be helped by putting greater emphasis on the interplay between moods and emotions.

6) What are the interpersonal causes and consequences of momentary affect at work (*new topic challenge*)?

The interpersonal or relational nature of affect has become apparent in recent years. Research has established that workers' feelings are regulated both unconsciously and consciously by the actions and feelings of their colleagues (e.g., Kelly & Barsade, 2001; Niven, Totterdell, & Holman, 2009; van Kleef, 2009), and that the exchange of emotions can have an impact on relationships and well-being (e.g., Rimé). However, our understanding of the relational aspects of momentary affect at work requires further development. There are a range of methods suitable for studying relationships in organizations, one of which is social network analysis (Borgatti & Foster, 2003; Totterdell, Wall, Holman, Diamond, & Epitropaki, 2004).

7) How can different types of affect measurement be integrated (*measurement challenge*)?

Emotion can be measured using different types of response (e.g., physiological, behavioral, self-report), but these responses often show low coherence (Mauss & Robinson, 2009). Greater understanding of how to reconcile data from different measures is therefore needed. This need is particularly pertinent because new opportunities are arising for collecting and integrating different sources of data from workers during work time (Wilhelm & Grossman, 2010). Portable recordings of physiological parameters (e.g., heart rate, blood pressure), movement, speech, geographic location, and visual environment are now feasible.

8) What analytic procedures are best suited to investigating temporal dynamics in affect (*analytic challenge*)?

Many traditional statistical techniques are based on assumptions of linear association, and are unable to adequately assess the temporal dynamics of momentary affect data. Developments in these techniques have emerged, for example dynamic mediated longitudinal analysis (Pitariu & Ployhart, 2010), but more are needed. Research would also benefit from greater use of computer simulation models. These would enable researchers to encapsulate and test their assumptions about how affective processes at work arise and develop over time (Farrell & Lewandowsky, 2010). Computational models are particularly suited to the study of temporal structure such as duration and rate of change, and allow for assessment of complex temporal dynamics in affect (Bosse, Pontier, & Treur, 2010).

9) What interventions are effective in enhancing momentary affect at work (*intervention challenge*)?

Few research studies have tested interventions that alter the causes of affect at work in order to change workers' affect and thereby influence behavioural outcomes. Intervention studies would be helpful for three reasons. First, they will help to establish that the associations between the supposed causes of affect and affect are causal rather than spurious. Second, they will confirm whether momentary associations translate into general ones (e.g., a worker may report feeling calmer when there is less time pressure but it does not necessarily follow that reducing time pressure will make the person feel calmer in general). Third, they have the potential to contribute positively to workers' well-being and organizational performance.

10) Can changes in momentary affect at work be sustained in the long-term (*sustainability challenge*)?

As we mentioned in the previous challenge, workplace interventions targeted at changing affect have the potential to enhance workers' well-being and performance. However, in light of the fact that individuals seem to return to their affect baseline even after very positive or negative events (e.g., Brickman, Coates, & Janoff-Pulman, 1978), it raises the question of whether interventions can enhance well-being and performance in the long-term. To achieve this, the interventions may need to be applied in particular ways, for example by varying their timing and enactment (Sheldon & Lyubomirsky, 2007). Research is needed to establish whether and how sustainable effects on momentary affect can be achieved in the workplace.

References

Alliger, G. M., & Williams, K. J. (1993). Using signal-contingent experience sampling methodology to study work in the field: A discussion and illustration examining task perceptions and mood. *Personnel Psychology, 46,* 525-549.

Allred, K. G., Mallozzi, J. S., Matsui, F., & Raia, C. P. (1997). The influence of anger and compassion on negotiation performance. *Organizational Behavior and Human Decision Processes, 70,* 175-187.

Amabile, T. M., Barsade, S. G., Mueller, J. S., & Staw, B. M. (2005). Affect and creativity at work. *Administrative Science Quarterly, 50,* 367–403.

Ambrose, M. L., Harland, L. K., & Kulik, C. T. (1991). Influence of social comparisons on perceptions of organizational fairness. *Journal of Applied Psychology, 76,* 239-246.

Andersson, L. M., & Pearson, C. M. (1999). Tit for tat? The spiraling effect of incivility in the workplace. *Academy of Management Review, 24,* 452-471.

Arnold, M. B. (1960). *Emotion and personality: Vol. 1. Psychological aspects.* New York, NY: Columbia University Press.

Ashkanasy, N. M., & Humphrey, R. H. (2011). Current emotion research in organizational behavior. *Emotion Review, 3,* 214-224.

Ashton-James, C. E., & Ashkanasy, N. M. (2005). What lies beneath? A process analysis of affective events theory. In N. M. Ashkanasy, W. J. Zerbe, & C. E. J. Hartel (Eds.). *Research on emotions in organizations, volume 1: The effect of affect in organizational settings* (pp. 23-46). Oxford, UK: Elsevier Science.

Averill, J. R. (1982). *Anger and aggression: An essay on emotion.* New York, NY: Springer-Verlag.

Bandura, A. (1977). *Self-efficacy: The exercise of control.* New York, NY: Freeman.

Barger, P., & Grandey, A. (2006). "Service with a smile" and encounter satisfaction: Emotional contagion and appraisal mechanisms. *Academy of Management Journal, 49,* 1229-1238.

Barsky, A., Kaplan, S. A., & Beal, D. J. (2011). Just feelings? The role of affect in the formation of organizational fairness judgments. *Journal of Management, 37,* 248-279.

Basch, J., & Fisher, C. D. (2000). Affective job events–emotions matrix: A classification of job related events and emotions experienced in the workplace. In N. Ashkanasy, W. Zerbe, & C. Hartel (Eds.), *Emotions in the workplace: Research, theory, and practice (pp. 36-48)*. Westport, CT: Quorum Books.

Baumeister, R. F., Bratslavsky, E., Finkenauer, C., & Vohs, K. D. (2001). Bad is stronger than good. *Review of General Psychology, 5*, 323-370.

Baumeister, R. F., Vohs, K., DeWall, C. N., & Zhang, L. (2007). How emotion shapes behavior: Feedback, anticipation and reflection, rather than direct causation. *Personality and Social Psychology Review, 11*, 167-203.

Beal, D. J., & Ghandour, L. (2011). Stability, change, and the stability of change in daily workplace affect. *Journal of Organizational Behavior, 32*, 526–546.

Beal, D. J., & Weiss, H. M. (2003). Methods of ecological momentary assessment in organizational research. *Organizational Research Methods, 6*, 440-464.

Beal, D. J., & Weiss, H. M. (2013). The episodic structure of life at work. In A. B. Bakker & K. Daniels (Eds.). *A day in the life of a happy worker*. Hove, UK: Psychology Press.

Beal, D. J., Weiss, H. M., Barros, E., & Macdermid, S. M. (2005). An episodic process model of affective influences on performance. *Journal of Applied Psychology, 90*, 1054-1068.

Begley, T. M. (1994). Expressed and suppressed anger as predictors of health complaints. *Journal of Organizational Behavior, 15*, 503-516.

Bies, R. J. (1987). The predicament of injustice: The management of moral outrage. In B. M. Staw & L. L. Cummings (Eds.), *Research in organizational behavior* (pp. 289-319). Greenwich, CT: JAI Press.

Bies, R. J., & Tripp, T. M. (1998). The many faces of revenge: The good, the bad, and the ugly. In R. W. Griffin, A. M. O'Leary-Kelly, & J. Collins (Eds.), *Dysfunctional behavior in organizations* (pp. 49-68). Greenwich, CT: JAI Press.

Binnewies, C., & Wörnlein, S. C. (2011). What makes a creative day? A diary study on the interplay between affect, job stressors, and job control. *Journal of Organizational Behavior, 32*, 589–607.

Bodenhausen, G. V., Sheppard, L. A., & Kramer, G. P. (1994). Negative affect and social judgment: The differential impact of anger and sadness. *European Journal of Social Psychology, 24*, 45-62.

Bolger, N., Davis, A., & Rafaeli, E. (2003). Diary methods: Capturing life as it is lived. *Annual Review of Psychology, 54*, 579-616.

Bono, J. E., & Ilies, R. (2006). Charisma, positive emotions and mood contagion. *The Leadership Quarterly, 17*, 317-334.

Borgatti, S. P., & Foster, P. C. (2003). The network paradigm in organizational research: A review and typology. *Journal of Management, 29,* 991-1013.

Bosse, T., Pontier, M., & Treur, J. (2010). A computational model based on Gross' emotion regulation theory. *Cognitive Systems Research, 11,* 211-230.

Bowling, N. A., Beehr, T. A., Wagner, S. H. & Libkuman, T. M. (2005). Adaptation-level theory, opponent process theory, and dispositions: An integrated approach to the stability of job satisfaction. *Journal of Applied Psychology, 90,* 1044–1053.

Brickman, P., Coates, D., & Janoff-Bulman, R. (1978). Lottery winners and accident victims: Is happiness relative? *Journal of Personality and Social Psychology, 36,* 917–927.

Brief, A. P., & Weiss, H. M. (2002). Organizational behavior: Affect in the workplace. *Annual Review of Psychology, 53,* 279–307.

Briner, R. B. (1999). The neglect and importance of emotion at work. *European Journal of Work and Organizational Psychology, 8,* 323-346.

Briner, R. B., & Kiefer, T. (2009). Whither psychological research into emotion at work? Feeling for the future. *International Journal of Work Organisation and Emotion, 3,* 161-173.

Brown, S. P., Westbrook, R. A., & Challagalla, G. (2005). Good cope, bad cope: Adaptive and maladaptive coping strategies following a critical negative work event. *Journal of Applied Psychology, 90,* 792-798.

Cacioppo, J. T., Berntson, G. G., Larsen, J. T., Poehlmann, K. M., & Ito, T. A. (2000). The psychophysiology of emotion. In Lewis, M., & Haviland-Jones, J. M. (Eds.), *The handbook of emotion.* New York, NY: Guildford Press.

Carver, C. S., & Scheier, M. F. (1990). Origins and functions of positive and negative affect: A control-process view. *Psychological Review, 97,* 19–35.

Cohen-Charash, Y. (2009). Episodic envy. *Journal of Applied Social Psychology, 39,* 2128-2173.

Coles, J., Koritsas, S., Boyle, M., & Stanley, J. (2007). GPs, violence and work performance: 'Just part of the job?'. *Australian Family Physician, 36,* 189-191.

Cropanzano, R., Weiss, H., Hale, J., & Reb, J. (2003). The structure of affect: Reconsidering the relationship between negative and positive affectivity. *Journal of Management, 29,* 831-857.

Csikszentmihalyi, M., & Larson, R. (1987). Validity and reliability of the experience-sampling method. *The Journal of Nervous and Mental Disease, 175,* 526-536.

Csikszentmihalyi, M., & LeFevre, J. (1989). Optimal experience in work and leisure. *Journal of Personality and Social Psychology, 56,* 815-822.

Damasio, A. R. (1994). *Descartes' error.* New York, NY: Grosset Putnam.

Dasborough, M. T. (2006). Cognitive asymmetry in employee emotional reactions to leadership behaviors. *The Leadership Quarterly, 17,* 163-178.

Darwin, C. (1872). *The expression of emotions in man and animals.* Chicago, IL: University of Chicago Press.

De Bono, J. E., Jackson Foldes, H., Vinson, G., & Muros, J. P. (2007). Workplace emotions: The role of supervision and leadership. *Journal of Applied Psychology, 92,* 1357-1367.

De Dreu, C. K. W., Giebels, E., & Van de Vliert, E. (1998). Social motives and trust in integrative negotiation: The disruptive effects of punitive capability. *Journal of Applied Psychology, 83,* 408-422.

Dimotakis, N., Scott, B. A., & Joopman, J. (2011). An experience sampling investigation of workplace interactions, affective states, and employee well-being. *Journal of Organizational Behavior, 32,* 527-588.

Domagalski, T. A., & Steelman, L. A. (2005). The impact of work events and disposition on the experience and expression of employee anger. *Organizational Analysis, 13,* 31-52.

Dunn, J. R., & Schweitzer, M. (2006). Green and mean: Envy and social undermining in organizations. In A. Tenbrunsel (Ed.), *Research on managing groups and teams: Ethics in groups* (pp. 177-197). Elsevier.

Eby, L. T., Maher, C., & Butts, M. (2010). The intersection of work and family life: The role of affect. *Annual Review of Psychology, 61,* 599-622.

Ekman, P. (1972). Universals and cultural differences in facial expressions of emotion. In J. Cole (Ed.), *Nebraska Symposium on Motivation, 1971* (Vol. 19, pp. 207-282). Lincoln: University of Nebraska Press.

Elfenbein, H. A. (2007). Emotion in organizations: A review and theoretical integration. *Academy of Management Annals, 1,* 371-457.

Eisenberg, J., & James, K. (2005). The relationship between affect and creativity in organizations: The roles of affect characteristics, neurocognitive mechanisms and task type. In N. M. Ashkanasy, W. J. Zerbe, & C. E. J. Hartel (Eds.). *Research on emotions in organizations, volume 1: The effect of affect in organizational settings* (pp. 241-261). Oxford, UK: Elsevier Science.

Eysenck, H. J. (1967). *The biological basis of personality.* Springfield, IL: Charles C Thomas.

Farrell, S., & Lewandowsky, S. (2010). Computational models as aids to better reasoning in psychology. *Current Directions in Psychological Science, 19*, 329-335.

Feldman Barrett, L. (2006). Emotions as natural kinds? *Perspectives on Psychological Science 10*, 20-46.

Feldman Barrett, L., Lindquist, K. A., Bliss-Moreau, E., Duncan, S., Gendron, M., Mize, J., & Brennan, L. (2007). Of mice and men. Natural kinds of emotions in the mammalian brain? A response to Panksepp and Izard. *Perspectives on Psychological Science, 2*, 297-312.

Fisher, C. D. (2000). Mood and emotions while working: Missing pieces of job satisfaction? *Journal of Organizational Behavior, 21*, 185–202.

Fisher, C. D. (2002). Antecedents and consequences of real-time affective reactions at work. *Motivation and Emotion, 26*, 3-30.

Fisher, C. D. (2003). Why do lay people believe that satisfaction and performance are correlated? Possible sources of a commonsense theory. *Journal of Organizational Behavior, 24*, 1–25.

Fisher, C. D. (2008). Emotions in and around performance: The thrill of victory, the agony of defeat. In N. M. Ashkanasy & C. L. Cooper (Eds.), *Research companion to emotion in organizations* (pp. 120-135). Cheltenham, UK: Edward Elgar.

Fisher, C. D. (2010). Happiness at work. *International Journal of Management Reviews, 12*, 384-412.

Fitness, J. (2000). Anger in the workplace: An emotion script approach to anger episodes between workers and their superiors, co-workers and subordinates. *Journal of Organizational Behavior, 21*, 147-162.

Forgas, J. P. (1995). Mood and judgment: The affect infusion model (AIM). *Psychological Bulletin, 117*, 39–66.

Fox, S., & Spector, P. E. (1999). A model of work frustration-aggression. *Journal of Organizational Behavior, 20*, 915-932.

Fredrickson, B. L. (2001). The role of positive emotions in positive psychology: The broaden-and-build theory of positive emotions. *American Psychologist, 56*, 218–226.

Fredrickson, B. L. (2013). Updated thinking on positivity ratios. *American Psychologist, 68*, 814-822.

Fredrickson, B. L., Mancuso, R. A., Branigan, C., & Tugade, M. M. (2000). The undoing effect of positive emotions. *Motivation and Emotion, 24*, 237-258.

Friedman, R., Olekalns, M., Anderson, C., Jeanne, B., Nathan, G., & Lisco, C. C. (2004). The positive and negative effects of anger on dispute resolution: Evidence from electronically mediated disputes. *Journal of Applied Psychology, 89,* 369-376.

Frijda, N. H. (1986). *The emotions.* Cambridge, UK: Cambridge University Press.

Frijda, N. H. (2010). Impulsive action and motivation. *Biological Psychology, 84,* 570-579.

Fritz, C., Sonnentag, S., Spector, P. E, & McInroe, J. A. (2010). The weekend matters: Relationships between stress recovery and affective experiences. *Journal of Organizational Behavior, 31,* 1137–1162.

Fuller, J. A., Stanton, J. M., Fisher, G. G., Spitzmüller, C., Russell, S. S., & Smith, P. C. (2003). A lengthy look at the daily grind: Time series analysis of events, mood, stress, and satisfaction. *Journal of Applied Psychology, 88,* 1019–1033.

Geddes, D., & Callister, R. R. (2007). Crossing the line(s): A dual threshold model of anger in organizations. *Academy of Management Review, 32,* 721-746.

George, J. M. (1989). Mood and absence. *Journal of Applied Psychology, 74,* 317–324.

George, J. (1991). State or trait: Effects of positive mood on prosocial behaviours at work. *Journal of Applied Psychology, 76,* 299-307.

George, J. (2011). Dual tuning: A minimum condition for understanding affect in organizations? *Organizational Psychology Review, 1,* 147-164.

George, J. M., & Brief, A. P. (1992). Feeling good-doing good: A conceptual analysis of the mood at work-organizational spontaneity relationship. *Psychological Bulletin, 112,* 310-329.

George, J. M., & Brief, A. P. (1996). Motivational agendas in the workplace: The effects of feelings on focus of attention and work motivation. *Research in Organizational Behavior, 19,* 75-109.

George, J. M., & Zhou, J. (2002). Understanding when bad moods foster creativity and good ones don't: The role of context and clarity of feelings. *Journal of Applied Psychology, 87,* 687-697.

Gibson, D. E., & Callister, R. R. (2010). Anger in organizations: Review and integration. *Journal of Management, 36,* 66-93.

Gibson, D. E., Schweitzer, M., Callister, R. R., & Gray, B. (2009). The influence of anger expressions on outcomes in organizations. *Negotiation and Conflict Management Research, 2,* 236-262.

Glomb, T. M. (2002). Workplace anger and aggression: Informing conceptual models with data from specific encounters. *Journal of Occupational Health Psychology, 7,* 20-36.

Glomb, T. M., Bhave, D. P., Miner, A. G., & Wall, M. (2011). Doing good, feeling good: Examining the role of organizational citizenship behaviors in changing mood. *Personnel Psychology, 64,* 191–223.

Glomb, T. M., & Hulin, C. L. (1997). Anger and gender effects in observed supervisor-subordinate dyadic interactions. *Organizational Behavior and Human Decision Processes, 72,* 281-307.

Gooty, J., Gavin, M., & Ashkanasy, N. M. (2009). Emotions research in OB: The challenges that lie ahead. *Journal of Organizational Behavior, 30,* 833-838.

Grandey, A. A. (2000). Emotional regulation in the workplace: A new way to conceptualize emotional labor. *Journal of Occupational Health Psychology, 5,* 95-110.

Grandey, A., Tam, A., & Brauburger, A. (2002). Affective states and traits in the workplace: Diary and survey data from young workers. *Motivation and Emotion, 26,* 31-55.

Gross, J. J. (1998). The emerging field of emotion regulation: An integrative review. *Review of General Psychology, 2,* 271-299.

Gross, J. (2010). The futures so bright, I gotta wear shades. *Emotion Review, 2,* 212-216.

Grube, A., Schroer, J., Hentzschel, C. & Hertel, G. (2008). The event reconstruction method: An efficient measure of experience-based job satisfaction. *Journal of Occupational and Organizational Psychology, 81,* 669-689.

Hart , P. M, Wearing, A. J., & Headey B. (1995). Police stress and well-being: Integrating personality, coping and daily work experiences. *Journal of Occupational and Organizational Psychology, 68,* 133–56

Harter, J. K., Schmidt, F. L., Asplund, J. W., Killham, E. A., & Agrawal, S. (2010). Causal impact of employee work perceptions on the bottom line of organizations. *Perspectives on Psychological Science, 5,* 378-389.

Hersey, R. B. (1932). *Workers' emotions in the shop and home: A study of individual workers from the psychological and physiological standpoint.* Philadelphia: University of Pennsylvania.

Hill, S. E., DelPriore, D., & Vaughan, P. W. (2011). The cognitive consequences of envy: Attention, memory, and self-regulatory depletion. *Journal of Personality and Social Psychology, 101,* 653-666.

Holman, D., Totterdell, P., & Rogelberg, S. G. (2005). A daily diary study of goal-striving: The relationship between goal distance, goal velocity, affect, expectancies and effort. In N. M. Ashkanasy, W. J. Zerbe, & C. E. J. Hartel (Eds.). *Research on emotions in organizations, volume 1: The effect of affect in organizational settings* (pp. 95-122). Oxford, UK: Elsevier Science.

Ilies, R., Dimotakis, N., & Watson, D. (2010). Mood, blood pressure, and heart rate at work: An experience-sampling study. *Journal of Occupational Health Psychology, 15*, 120-130.

Ilies, R., Scott, B. A., & Judge, T. A. (2006). The interactive effects of personal traits and experienced states on intraindividual patterns of citizenship behaviour. *Academy of Management Journal, 49*, 561-575.

Ilies, R., Wegner, D. T., & Morgeson, F. P. (2007). Explaining affective linkages in teams: Individual differences in susceptibility to contagion and individualism-collectivism. *Journal of Applied Psychology, 92*, 1140-1148.

Janssen, O., Lam, C. K., & Huang, X. (2010). Emotional exhaustion and job performance: The moderating roles of distributive justice and positive affect. *Journal of Organizational Behavior, 31*, 787–809.

Judge, T. A., & Bono, J. E. (2001). Relationship of core self-evaluations traits – self-esteem, generalized self-efficacy, locus of control, and emotional stability – with job satisfaction and job performance: A meta-analysis. *Journal of Applied Psychology, 86*, 80–92.

Judge, T. A., & Ilies, R. (2004). Affect and job satisfaction: A study of their relationship at work and at home. *Journal of Applied Psychology, 89*, 661–673.

Judge, T. A., & Kammeyer-Mueller, J. D. (2008). Affect, satisfaction, and performance. In N. M. Ashkanasy & C. L. Cooper (Eds.), *Research companion to emotion in organizations* (pp. 136-151). Cheltenham, UK: Edward Elgar.

Kahneman, D., Krueger, A. B., Schkade, D. A., Schwarz, N., & Stone, A. A. (2004). A survey method for characterizing daily life experience: The day reconstruction method. *Science, 306*, 1776–1780.

Kanfer, R., & Stubblebine, P. C. (2008). Affect and work motivation. In N. M. Ashkanasy & C. L. Cooper (Eds.), *Research companion to emotion in organizations* (pp. 170-182). Cheltenham, UK: Edward Elgar.

Kanner, A. D., Coyne, J. C., Schaefer, C., & Lazarus, R. S. (1981). Comparison of two modes of stress measurement: Daily hassles and uplifts versus major life events. *Journal of Behavioral Medicine, 4*, 1–39.

Kelly, J. R., & Barsade, S. G. (2001). Moods and emotions in small groups and work teams. *Organizational Behavior and Human Decision Processes, 86*, 99-130.

Keltner, D., & Kring, A. M. (1998). Emotion, social function, and psychopathology. *Review of General Psychology, 2*, 320-342.

Kuller, R., Ballal, S., Laike, T., Mikellides, B., & Tonello, G. (2006). The impact of light and colour on psychological mood: A cross-cultural study of indoor work environments. *Ergonomics, 49*, 1496-1507.

Kuppens, P., & Tong, E. M. W. (2010). An appraisal account of individual differences in emotional experiences. *Social and Personality Psychology Compass, 4*, 1138-1150.

Lawrence, S (2008). The case for emotion-induced toxicity: Making sense of toxic emotions in the workplace. In N. M. Ashkanasy & C. L. Cooper (Eds.), *Research companion to emotion in organizations* (pp. 73-89). Cheltenham, UK: Edward Elgar.

Lazarus, R. S. (1991). *Emotion and adaptation.* New York: Oxford University Press.

Lazarus, R. S., & Lazarus, B. N. (1994). *The emotional dramas of everyday life: Understanding and managing them.* New York, NY: Oxford University Press.

Lerner, J. S., & Tiedens, L. Z. (2006). Portrait of the angry decision maker: How appraisal tendencies shape anger's influence on cognition. *Journal of Behavioral Decision Making, 19*, 115-137.

Lewis, K. M. (2000). When leaders display emotion: How followers respond to negative emotional expression of male and female leaders. *Journal of Organizational Behavior, 21*, 221-234.

Lyubomirsky, S., King, L. A., & Diener, E. (2005). The benefits of frequent positive affect: Does happiness lead to success? *Psychological Bulletin, 131*, 803–855.

Madjar N, Oldham G. R., & Pratt, M. G. (2002). There's no place like home: The contributions of work and non-work creativity support to employees' creative performance. *Academy of Management Journal, 45*, 757-767.

Manucia, G. K., Baumann, D. J., & Cialdini, R. B. (1984). Mood influences on helping: Direct effects or side effects? *Journal of Personality and Social Psychology, 46*, 357-364.

Mauss, I., & Robinson, M. D. (2009). Measures of emotion: A review. *Cognition and Emotion, 23*, 209-237.

Mayer, J., & Salovey, P. (1997). What is emotional intelligence? In P. Salovey & D. Sluyter (Eds.), *Emotional development and emotional intelligence: Implications for educators* (pp. 3–31). New York, NY: Basic Books.

Miner, A. G., & Glomb, T. M. (2010). State mood, task performance, and behavior at work: A within-persons approach. *Organizational Behavior and Human Decision Processes, 112,* 43–57.

Miner, A. G., Glomb, T. M., & Hulin, C. (2005). Experience sampling mood and its correlates at work. *Journal of Occupational and Organizational Psychology, 78,* 171–193.

Miner, F. C. (1990). Jealousy on the job. *Personnel Journal, 69,* 88-95.

Miron-Spektor, E., Efrat-Treister, D., Rafaeli, A. & Schwartz-Cohen, O. (2011). Others' anger makes people work harder not smarter: The effect of observing anger and sarcasm on complex thinking. *Journal of Applied Psychology, 96,* 1065-1075.

Miron-Spektor, E., & Rafaeli, A. (2009). The effects of anger in the workplace: When, where and why observing anger enhances or hinders performance. *Research in Personnel and Human Resource Management, 28,* 153-178.

Mittal, V., & Ross, W. T. (1998). The impact of positive and negative affect and issue framing on issue interpretation and risk taking. *Organizational Behavior and Human Decision Processes, 76,* 298–324.

Motowidlo, S. J., Packard, J. S., & Manning, M. R. (1986). Occupational stress - its causes and consequences for job-performance. *Journal of Applied Psychology, 71,* 618-629.

Natale, S. M., Campana, C., & Sora, S. A. (1988). How envy affects management. *International Journal of Technology Management, 3,* 543-556.

Ng, C. K., & Wong, K. F. E. (2008). Emotion and organizational decision-making: The roles of negative affect and anticipated regret in making decisions under escalation conditions. In N. M. Ashkanasy & C. L. Cooper (Eds.), *Research companion to emotion in organizations* (pp. 45-60). Cheltenham, UK: Edward Elgar.

Niven, K., Totterdell, P., & Holman, D. (2009). A classification of controlled interpersonal affect regulation strategies. *Emotion, 9,* 498-509.

Parkinson, B. (1995). *Ideas and realities of emotion.* London, UK: Routledge.

Parkinson, R. (1996). Emotions are social. *British Journal of Psychology, 87,* 663-683.

Parkinson, B., Briner, R. B., Reynolds, S., & Totterdell, P. (1995). Time frames for mood: Relations between momentary and generalized ratings of affect. *Personality and Social Psychology Bulletin, 21,* 331-339.

Parkinson, B., Totterdell, P., Briner, R. B., & Reynolds, S. (1996). *Changing moods: The psychology of mood and mood regulation.* Harlow: Longman.

Parks, C. D., Rumble, A. C., & Posey, D. C. (2002). The effects of envy on reciprocation in a social dilemma. *Personality and Social Psychology Bulletin, 28,* 509-520.

Penney, L., & Spector, P. E. (2008). Emotions and counterproductive work behavior. In N. M. Ashkanasy & C. L. Cooper (Eds.), *Research companion to emotion in organizations* (pp. 183-196). Cheltenham, UK: Edward Elgar.

Pitariu, A. H., & Ployhart, R. E. (2010). Explaining change: Theorizing and testing dynamic mediated longitudinal relationships. *Journal of Management, 36,* 405-429.

Pugh, S. D. (2001). Service with a smile: Emotional contagion in the service encounter. *Academy of Management Journal, 44,* 1018-1027.

Rank, J., & Frese, M. (2008). The impact of emotions, moods and other affect-related variables on creativity, innovation, and initiative. In N. M. Ashkanasy & C. L. Cooper (Eds.), *Research companion to emotion in organizations* (pp. 103-119). Cheltenham, UK: Edward Elgar.

Rau, R., & Triemer, A. (2004). Overtime in relation to blood pressure and mood during work, leisure, and night time. *Social Indicators Research, 67,* 51-73.

Repetti, R. L. (1993). Short-term effects of occupational stressors on daily mood and health complaints. *Health Psychology, 12,* 125-131

Richard, E. M., & Diefendorff, J. M. (2011). Self-regulation during a single performance episode: Mood-as-information in the absence of formal feedback. *Organizational Behavior and Human Decision Processes, 115,* 99–110.

Rimé, B. (2009). Emotion elicits the social sharing of emotion: Theory and empirical review. *Emotion Review, 1,* 60-85.

Rozin, P., & Royzman, E. B. (2001). Negativity bias, negativity dominance, and contagion. *Personality and Social Psychology Review, 5,* 296-320.

Sauter, K. (2010). More than happy: The need for disentangling positive emotions. *Current Directions in Psychological Science, 19,* 36-40.

Schaubroeck, J., & Lam, S. S. K. (2004). Comparing lots before and after: Promotion rejectees' invidious reactions to promotees. *Organizational Behavior and Human Decision Processes, 94,* 33-47.

Schaufeli, W. B., & Bakker, A. B. (2010). Defining and measuring work engagement: Bringing clarity to the concept. In A. B. Bakker & M. P. Leiter (Eds.), *Work engagement: A handbook of essential theory and research* (pp.10-24). New York: Psychology Press.

Scheier, M. F., & Carver, C. S. (1985). Optimism, coping, and health: Assessment and implications of generalized outcome expectancies. *Health Psychology, 4,* 219-247.

Schwarz, N., & Clore, G. L. (1983). Mood, misattribution and judgments of well-being: Informative and directive functions of affective states. *Journal of Personality and Social Psychology, 45,* 513-523.

Seo, M., Bartunek, J. M., & Feldman Barrett, L. (2010). The role of affective experience in work motivation: Test of a conceptual model. *Journal of Organizational Behavior, 31,* 951-968.

Sheldon, K. M., & Lyubomirsky, S. (2007). Is it possible to become happier? (And if so, how?). *Social and Personality Psychology Compass, 1,* 129–145.

Shirom, A. (2001). Vigor as a positive affect at work: Conceptualizing vigor, its relations with related constructs, and its antecedents and consequences. *Review of General Psychology, 15,* 50-64.

Sinclair, M., Ashkanasy, N. M., & Chattopadhyay, P. (2010). Affective antecedents of intuitive decision-making. *Journal of Management and Organization, 6,* 382-398.

Smith, R. H., Kim, S. H., & Parrott, W. G. (1988). Envy and jealousy semantic problems and experiential distinctions. *Personality and Social Psychology Bulletin, 14,* 401-409.

Spector, P. E., & Fox, S. (2002). An emotion-centered model of voluntary work behavior: Some parallels between counterproductive work behavior and organizational citizenship behavior. *Human Resource Management Review, 12,* 269-292.

Spence, J. R., Ferris, D. L., Brown, D. J., & Heller, D. (2011). Understanding daily citizenship behaviors: A social comparison perspective. *Journal of Organizational Behavior, 32,* 547–571.

Staw, B. M., & Barsade S. G. (1993). Affect and managerial performance: A test of the sadder-but-wiser vs. happier-and-smarter hypotheses. *Administrative Science Quarterly, 38,* 304–328.

Staw, B. M., Sutton, R. I., & Pelled, L. H. (1994). Employee positive emotion and favorable outcomes at the workplace. *Organization Science, 5,* 51–71.

Stone, A. A, Hedges, S. M., Neale, J. M, & Satin, M. S. (1985). Prospective and cross-sectional mood reports offer no evidence of a "blue Monday" phenomenon. *Journal of Personality and Social Psychology, 49,* 129-134

Stone, A. A., Smyth, J. M., Pickering, T., & Schwartz, J. (1996). Daily mood variability: Form of diurnal patterns and determinants of diurnal patterns. *Journal of Applied Social Psychology, 26,* 1286–1305.

Sy, T., Côté, S., & Saavedra, R. (2005). The contagious leader: Impact of the leader's mood on the mood of group members, group affective tone, and group processes. *Journal of Applied Psychology, 90,* 295–305.

Tafrate, R. C., Kassinove, H., & Dundin, L. (2002). Anger episodes in high- and low-trait anger community adults. *Journal of Clinical Psychology, 58,* 1573-1591.

Teuchmann, K., Totterdell, P., & Parker, S. K. (1999). Rushed, unhappy, and drained: An experience sampling study of relations between time pressure, perceived control, mood, and emotional exhaustion in a group of accountants. *Journal of Occupational Health Psychology, 4,* 37-54.

Tesser, A. (1991). Emotion in social comparison and reflection processes. In J.Suls & T. A.Wills (Eds.), *Social comparison: Contemporary theory and research* (pp. 115-145). Hillsdale, NJ: Lawrence Erlbaum.

Totterdell, P. (1995). The effects of depressed affect on diurnal and ultradian variations in mood in a healthy sample. *Chronobiology International, 12,* 278-289.

Totterdell, P. (1999). Mood scores: Mood and performance in professional cricketers. *British Journal of Psychology, 90,* 317-332.

Totterdell, P. (2000). Catching moods and hitting runs: Mood linkage and subjective performance in professional sport teams. *Journal of Applied Psychology, 85,* 848-859.

Totterdell, P., & Holman, D. (2003). Emotion regulation in customer service roles: Testing a model of emotional labor. *Journal of Occupational Health Psychology, 8,* 55-73.

Totterdell, P., Kellett, S., Teuchmann, K., & Briner, R. B. (1998). Evidence of mood linkage in work groups. *Journal of Personality and Social Psychology, 74,* 1504-1515.

Totterdell, P., & Parkinson, B. (1999). Use and effectiveness of self-regulation strategies for improving mood in a group of trainee teachers. *Journal of Occupational Health Psychology, 4,* 219-232.

Totterdell, P., Spelten, E. R., Smith, L. R., Barton, J., & Folkard, S. (1995). On-shift and daily variations in self report and performance measures in rotating-shift and permanent night nurses. *Work & Stress, 9,* 187-197.

Totterdell, P., Wall, T., Holman, D., Diamond, H., & Epitropaki, O. (2004). Affect networks: A structural analysis of the relationship between work ties and job-related affect. *Journal of Applied Psychology, 89*, 854-867.

Totterdell, P., Wood, S., & Wall, T. (2006). An intraindividual test of the demands-control model: A weekly diary study of job strain in portfolio workers. *Journal of Occupational and Organizational Psychology, 79*, 63-84.

Van de Ven, N., Zeelenberg, M., & Pieters, R. (2009). Leveling up and down: The experience of benign and malicious envy. *Emotion, 9*, 419-429.

Van de Ven, N., Zeelenberg, M., & Pieters, R. (2010). Warding off the evil eye: When the fear of being envied increases prosocial behavior. *Psychological Science, 21*, 1671-1677.

Van de Ven, N., Zeelenberg, M., & Pieters, R. (2011). Why envy outperforms admiration. *Personality and Social Psychology Bulletin, 37*, 784-795.

Van Kleef, G. A. (2009). How emotions regulate social life: The emotions as social information (EASI) model. *Current Directions in Psychological Science, 18*, 184-188.

Van Kleef, G. A., De Dreu, C. K. W., & Manstead, A. S. R. (2004). The interpersonal effects of anger and happiness in negotiations. *Journal of Personality and Social Psychology, 86*, 57-76.

Van Kleef, G. A., De Dreu, C. K. W., Pietroni, D., & Manstead, A. S. R. (2006). Power and emotions in negotiation: Power moderates the interpersonal effects of anger and happiness on concession making. *European Journal of Social Psychology, 36*, 557-581.

Van Knippenberg, D., Kooij-de Bode, H. J. M., & van Ginkel, W. P. (2010). The interactive effects of mood and trait negative affect in group decisions. *Organization Science, 21*, 731-744.

Vecchio, R. P. (1995). It's not easy being green: Jealousy and envy in the workplace. In G. R.Ferris (Ed.), *Research in personnel and human resources management* (Vol. 13, pp. 201-244). Stanford, CT: JAI Press.

Vecchio, R. P. (2000). Negative emotion in the workplace: Employee jealousy and envy. *International Journal of Stress Management, 7*, 161-179.

Vecchio, R. P. (2005). Explorations in employee envy: Feeling envious and feeling envied. *Cognition and Emotion, 19*, 69-81.

Verduyn, P., Delvaux, E., van Coillie, H., Tuerlinckx, F., & van Mechelen, I. (2009). Predicting the duration of emotional experience: Two experience sampling studies. *Emotion, 9*, 83-91.

Wagner, D. T., & Ilies, R. (2008). Affective influences on employee satisfaction and performance. In N. M. Ashkanasy & C. L. Cooper (Eds.), *Research companion to emotion in organizations* (pp. 152-169). Cheltenham, UK: Edward Elgar.

Walter, F., & Bruch, H. (2009). An affective events model of charismatic leadership behavior: A review, theoretical integration, and research agenda. *Journal of Management, 35,* 1428-1452.

Watson, D., Wiese, D., Vaidya, J., & Tellegen, A. (1999). The two general activation systems of affect: Structural findings, evolutionary considerations, and psychobiological evidence. *Journal of Personality and Social Psychology, 76,* 820-838.

Weiss, H. M., & Beal, D. J. (2005). Reflections on affective events theory. In N. M. Ashkanasy, W. J. Zerbe, & C. E. J. Hartel (Eds.). *Research on emotions in organizations, volume 1: The effect of affect in organizational settings* (pp. 1-21). Oxford, UK: Elsevier Science.

Weiss, H. M., & Brief, A. P. (2001). Affect at work: A historical perspective. In R. Payne & C. Cooper (Eds.), *Emotions at work: Theory, research and applications in management* (pp. 133-172). Chichester, England: Wiley.

Weiss, H. M., & Cropanzano, R. (1996). Affective events theory: A theoretical discussion of the structure, causes and consequences of affective experiences at work. *Research in Organizational Behavior, 18,* 1–74.

Weiss, H. M., Nicholas, J. P., & Daus, C. S. (1999). An examination of the joint effects of affective experiences and job beliefs on job satisfaction and variations in affective experiences over time. *Organizational Behavior and Human. Decision Processeses, 78,* 1–24

Weiss, H. M. & Rupp, D. E. (2011). Experiencing work: An essay on a person-centric work psychology. *Industrial and Organizational Psychology: Perspectives on Science and Practice, 4,* 83-97.

Wheeler, L., & Reis, H. T. (1991). Self-recording of everyday life events: Origins, types, and uses. *Journal of Personality, 59,* 339-354.

Wilhelm, F. H., & Grossman, P. (2010). Emotions beyond the laboratory: Theoretical fundaments, study design, and advanced analytic strategies for advanced ambulatory assessment. *Biological Psychology, 84,* 552-569.

Williams, K. J., & Alliger, G. M. (1994). Role stressors, mood spillover, and perceptions of work-family conflict in employed parents. *Academy of Management Journal, 37,* 837-868.

Williams, K.J., Suls J., Alliger, G. M., Learner, S. M., & Wan, C. K. (1991). Multiple role juggling and daily mood states in working mothers: An experience sampling study. *Journal of Applied Psychology, 76,* 664–674.

Yerkes, R. M., & Dodson, J. D. (1908). The relation of strength of stimulus to rapidity of habit-formation. *Journal of Comparative Neurology and Psychology, 18,* 459-482.

Zajonc, R. B. (1980). Feelings and thinking: Preferences need no inferences. *American Psychologist, 35,* 151-175.

Zohar, D. (1999). When things go wrong: The effect of daily work hassles on effort, exertion and negative mood. *Journal of Occupational and Organizational Psychology, 72,* 265–83.